Germany 1815–1939

The rise of nationalism

Finlay McKichan

For Fiona

Oliver & Boyd
Pearson Education Limited
Edinburgh Gate
Harlow
Essex CM20 2JE
An imprint of Longman Group UK Ltd

First published 1992
Sixth impression 1999

British Library Cataloguing in Publication Data

McKichan, Finlay
    Germany, 1815–1939: Rise of Nationalism. –
    (Higher Grade History Series)
    I. Title   II. Series
    943

    ISBN 0–05–005081–8

Illustrated by Hardlines
Set in 10/12 Bembo Linotron
Printed in Singapore (COS)

The Publisher's policy is to use paper manufactured from sustainable
forests.

Contents

Introduction

Nationalism is the desire of people who believe that they have a common homeland, language and history to assert their rights against other nations and (if they have not already done so) to achieve unity and independence. It has been one of the great driving forces of European and world history in the nineteenth and twentieth centuries.

This book is about the growth of German nationalism and about the German state which was created in 1871 and how it changed between then and the outbreak of the Second World War in 1939.

In the revised Higher course three themes run through all the sections on Later Modern History. These are:

- *Ideology* – This means a set of ideas in which a group of people believe. These shared ideas affect the way in which they see themselves and the way in which they see other people.
- *Identity* – This means that people have a sense of belonging to a particular group or class or district or nation.
- *Authority* – This means something which either forces or persuades people to obey.

To make it easier to recognise these themes, you will be told near the beginning of each chapter how the themes run through it.

Each chapter is about some issue related to the growth of German nationalism or the German state. These are issues which historians and others have thought important enough to study, think about and discuss. You also will be asked to study, think about and discuss them. At the beginning of each chapter is a task, which suggests how you can approach the issue dealt with in the chapter. You may work individually or in a group. The issue will be divided into sub-issues to make it easier to follow. You will think about extracts from contemporary sources and modern historians, and about statistics, tables, maps, pictures and photos. The purpose of each chapter is to help you to come to conclusions, often in discussion or in a debate with your fellow students. After you have done these things you will find at the end of each chapter a set of essay titles. These will allow you to practise the skills you will need in the examination (especially in Paper 1 and in the Extended essay).

Setting the scene

Fig 0.1 Young people at the Brandenburg Gate celebrating the opening of the Berlin Wall in November 1989.

In the autumn of 1989 huge crowds demonstrated in the streets of East German cities such as Berlin, Dresden and Leipzig. They were demanding the end of forty-four years of communist rule in East Germany. Within weeks the communist government had fallen, and amazing scenes were occurring in Berlin. Young East Germans climbed to precarious positions on the Brandenburg Gate, which marked the border between the eastern and western zones of what had once been the capital city of Germany. They shouted and cheered to celebrate the fact that they could now walk through the border whenever they wanted to visit the west. Risking serious injury, they threw down with their bare hands the Berlin Wall, which for almost thirty years had separated the two zones and prevented all but the bravest or most foolhardy from escaping to the west. Figure 0.1 will give you an idea of the excitement of these days in 1989.

Less than a year later, on 3 October 1990, East and West Germany were reunited with solemn ceremony. People throughout Europe followed these events with rapt attention. They felt they were watching history unfold. For almost forty-five years the frontiers and governments of east and central Europe had been frozen in the 'Cold War' between the USSR and the West. What was happening in 1989 was the collapse of the Soviet Empire. In earlier decades the tanks of the Red Army would have rolled in (and sometimes did) to extinguish any opposition to communist rule. They were able to do so because the enormous contribution that the USSR had made to the defeat of Nazi Germany in 1945 had left eastern Europe under Russian control.

The events of 1945 in eastern Europe were like the scenes of titanic struggle and awful destruction referred to in ancient German legend – 'Gotterdammerung' or 'The Twilight of the Gods'. Germany had invaded Russia in 1941 with the aim of finding 'living space' for the German race and establishing 'an empire which would last 1000 years'. If you visit Germany or Austria today, you can see on war memorials the huge numbers of German soldiers who died 'in Russland' (in Russia) trying to establish this empire. The Russians lost 20 million people in what they call 'The Great Patriotic War'. When they finally fought their way into East Germany in 1945 and met up with American, British and French armies advancing from the west, they were determined that this would never happen again. Germany would never be allowed again to grow so powerful that she could invade her neighbours. This would be ensured by keeping her divided into two parts, which became the Federal German Republic (in the west) and the German Democratic Republic (in the east). Not only the GDR, but also the other countries of eastern Europe would be 'satellite states' under the control of the Soviet Union to ensure there was a broad buffer to protect the USSR from any new danger of invasion from the west. Now the satellite states are independent countries and Germany is reunited.

The German state which was split in 1945 had not in fact been united for very long. There had been a united Germany only since 1871. However, in these seventy or so years, her neighbours had come to feel that Germany had a dangerously inflated opinion of her own prestige and power. This nationalism, they felt, had been a major reason for the two world wars in the twentieth century.

What kind of Germany is now being rebuilt? Its population, natural resources, wealth and location at the centre of Europe will make a united Germany into a formidably powerful nation (see Figure 0.2). How will that power be used? Will Germany once again become a nationalist state seen as a threat by its neighbours? Chancellor Kohl said on reunification day in 1990 that this would not be so. This time there would be 'no restless Reich [empire]'. Instead, will Germany in the twenty-first century be a pillar of the

Key
- ———— Germany
- G.D.R. German Democratic Republic
- F.G.R. Federal German Republic
- D Denmark
- N Netherlands
- B Belgium

Fig 0.2   Europe in 1989.

European Community, using its energies to extend the community's powers and to incorporate in the community the former communist nations of eastern Europe? Has narrow German nationalism run its course? Did it really die in the ruins of Hitler's Third Reich in 1945?

Many people will be seeking answers to these questions in the years ahead. To understand the questions and the fears, we must go back about 200 years to the beginnings of German nationalism.

The origins of German nationalism

A nation can be described as a people who believe that they have a common homeland, a common language, and common history and traditions. In the eighteenth century this had been true of France and England for a very long time. Italy and Germany were more difficult cases. The Italians and the Germans certainly had their own languages and traditions. However, Italy was divided up among several rulers (some of whom were not Italian). The Germans were divided among a much larger number of rulers, and they were mixed in among other peoples over large areas of eastern Europe. The French Revolution in 1789 started a sequence of events through which Italians and Germans (and many other peoples in Europe and throughout the world) began to long for the day when their own nations would be united and independent from foreign rule.

We can find out why this happened and what the consequences were in Germany by thinking about several issues:

1. Why did the French Revolution make people throughout Europe more aware of belonging to a particular nation?
2. How was nationalism encouraged at this time by the work of thinkers, writers and artists?
3. What was Germany like in 1800 and how was it affected by Napoleon?

These issues raise questions about the *ideology* and *authority* of the French revolutionaries and the sense of *identity* of other European peoples, especially the Germans.

TASK

Imagine that you are a Prussian schoolteacher.

The year is 1813. You were a student when the French Revolution began in 1789 and you were very enthusiastic about the promises that the revolutionaries were making.

Now write a letter to a friend explaining:

1. why you were at first so enthusiastic about the French Revolution, but were later disappointed by it.

2. why you have become more and more proud of being German.

3. why you resent the way the Emperor Napoleon has treated Germany in general and Prussia in particular, and why you hope that Napoleon will be defeated in the great battles which are expected soon.

Nationalism in early nineteenth-century Europe
The French Revolution

On 14 July 1789 a Paris mob burst into the Bastille fortress and released the prisoners, some of whom had been kept there for many years because they had offended the government of King Louis XVI. It was not a very difficult fortress to storm, but the event was a powerful symbol.

Its message was announced to the world in the Declaration of the Rights of Man, which was adopted by the French National Assembly on 26 August. This stated that 'men are born and remain free and equal in rights. These rights are liberty, property, security and resistance to oppression.' People had the right to say and print what they thought. They should not be imprisoned simply because some powerful person ordered it. The law should treat everybody fairly.

These were powerful claims in a country in which the king had always ruled as he wished – on the grounds that he had been appointed by God to do so – and in which landowners at local level had almost complete control over the lives of ordinary people. The right to rule now belonged not to the king or to the landowners, but to the nation. What was more, these rights were claimed, not only for the French, but for all nations.

These events in Paris caused excitement throughout Europe. People were soon speaking of 'the revolution in France'. A common reaction was that of the English poet William

Wordsworth, who wrote, 'Bliss was it in that dawn to be alive, but to be young was very heaven.' There was a feeling that, not only in France but throughout Europe, things could never be the same again.

For some people in other countries the blissful dawn öffered by the French Revolution had already gone by 1793. By then France had become a republic, and the king and his family had been executed by the guillotine, to be followed during the Terror by many others who were aristocrats or merely enemies of those in power in Paris. By then also, the French Republic was at war with Britain, Austria, Prussia and Spain, and men of property feared invasion by French armies which were notorious for stealing whatever was worth taking.

But for others the prospect offered by the French Revolution was still pleasing. Towards the end of 1792, as the French armies won their first victories against Austria and Prussia, France promised 'fraternity and assistance' to all peoples who wanted liberty. Wherever French armies were victorious, there the power of landowners and wealthy churchmen would be ended. Among many people, therefore, the arrival of French revolutionary armies aroused great expectations.

The French did indeed turn out to be very good at ending the power of landowners and churchmen in the lands they conquered. In this sense they delivered the 'equality' they promised. The wealthy merchant might now feel every bit as good as the landowner. More difficult in the lands over which the French armies won control was the promise that the right to rule belonged to the nation. Some of these lands (for example, the Rhineland to the east and Savoy to the south-east) actually became part of France in the 1790s. This suggested at an early stage that France was more concerned for herself than for other nations. Other lands were theoretically independent, but obviously controlled by France. When Napoleon Bonaparte became the ruler of France (as First Consul in 1799 and then as Emperor in 1804), he even gave some of these lands to members of his family as kingdoms (for example, Holland to Louis Bonaparte, Westphalia to Jerome, Naples and then Spain to Joseph). Whether the lands conquered by the French had a French king or not, they all had to follow French orders. As Napoleon put it, 'My policy is France before all.' They all had to observe Napoleon's 'Continental system' by refusing to trade with Britain, his most constant enemy. The result was that they were poorer, short of vital commodities, and sometimes even starving. They all had to supply troops for Napoleon's Grand Army, and in 1812 saw their men march off to die in the wastes of eastern Europe when he decided to invade Russia.

Most people in Europe probably resented the sufferings, but they did not think any more deeply about the meaning of events.

As a famous German historian, Golo Mann, puts it:

> 'Most Germans probably tilled the land as they always had and only occasionally looked up from the plough when a neighbour told them . . . that the Emperor Napoleon had set out for Russia with an army the like of which had never been seen before.'
>
> (*The History of Germany Since 1789*)

However, people who did think about such things were very struck by the contradiction between French theory and French practice. Such people were likely to approve of the theory of the French revolutionaries – that the right to rule (sovereignty) belonged to the nation. And they were very conscious that in the most important matters sovereignty was actually being kept in France and was not being given to their own nation. The French had raised their expectations of controlling the destiny of their own nation, but had failed to deliver. David Thomson has explained this development in this way:

> 'It was only when populations found French masters no less exacting than their old regimes that they were fired to ideas of self-government. The idea that "sovereignty of the people" should lead to national independence was the indirect result of French occupation: its original meaning, of abolishing privilege and universalising rights, came to merge into this new implication only as a result of conquests. The French revolutionaries spread liberalism by intention but created nationalism by inadvertence'.

Nationalism

This sense of grievance against France was the beginning of a new concern for the rights of nations in the early nineteenth century. The excitement raised by French promises and the disillusionment caused by French domination encouraged some Italians and Germans to long for the day when their nations would be united and free from foreign rule. Most Italians and Germans may not have thought this way in the early 1800s, but the numbers of those who did were to grow and to become more powerful, and eventually they put the unification of Italy and Germany among the most important political developments of nineteenth-century Europe.

Their example encouraged other subjugated and divided nations in Europe and around the world. The word 'Nationalism' came to be used to express the desire of nations to assert their rights against other nations or groups, and in particular to achieve unity and independence if they had not already done so. Nationalism became one of the great driving forces of world history in the nineteenth and twentieth centuries.

Of course the causes of such great movements are many and varied. All this did not happen just because the promises of the French revolutionaries to the rest of Europe were not honoured. In Germany and elsewhere people were influenced not only by the actions of statesmen and generals, but also by the work of thinkers, writers and artists.

The Romantic movement

The thinkers and artists of the second half of the eighteenth century had been influenced by an intellectual movement called 'The Enlightenment'. They asked the questions 'What good does it do?' 'How useful is it?' about all human institutions.

In France the people who asked such questions found the old ways of doing things sadly lacking, and the French Revolution was the most dramatic result of the Enlightenment. But when writers and artists saw the consequences of the French Revolution, they tended to be less impressed by the questions the Enlightenment encouraged them to ask. For example, the German composer Beethoven at first dedicated his Eroica Symphony to Napoleon, but scored out the dedication in disgust in 1804 when Napoleon made himself emperor.

Beethoven was one of the greatest examples of the new 'Romantic movement' among artists and writers. The Romantics believed that the emotions you felt counted for more than logical questions. For inspiration they often turned away from the disappointing actions of people in their own day to grand but remote landscapes (such as the English Lake District, the basis of many of Wordsworth's poems) or to remote and heroic times.

In Germany legends of early German heroes became very popular. For example, the songs of the Nibelung told of ancient heroes such as Siegfried, who fought valiant battles by the River Rhine and who, when they were killed, were carried by the Valkyrie to Valhalla, the land of the fallen heroes. In 1808, at the height of Napoleon's power, Arnim and Brentano published a collection of old German ballads and folk tales under the title *The Boy's Magic Horn*. It contained many stories of German heroism, particularly from the Middle Ages (which much interested Romantic writers and artists). In Figure 1.1 you will see the title page of this book.

Even more famous were the Grimm brothers, who published their first books of German folk-tales in the years immediately before Napoleon's fall in 1815. Jakob Grimm explained: 'I strove to penetrate into the wild forests of our ancestors, listening to their whole language and watching their pure customs.'

None of these authors had political programmes or political ambitions. However, they were encouraging fellow Germans to think of earlier times when, they believed, Germans had played a more heroic role. By implication, they were suggesting that

Fig 1.1   The title page of The Boy's Magic Horn.

things could be different from the present, when Napoleon appeared to be able to march at will to and fro across Germany and when the Germans tended to be despised as soldiers.

The way in which soldiers of other nations despised the Germans is shown in this extract from *War and Peace* by the Russian novelist, Tolstoy. In it a retired Russian general is claiming that Napoleon is not as good a commander as most people think and that the Russians can beat him. His argument is that:

> '[Napoleon] began by attacking Germans and one would have to be half asleep not to beat the Germans. They never beat anyone – except one another. He made his reputation fighting against them.'

We will now consider where the Germans were to be found; how Germany was organised in the early nineteenth century; and the impact of the French armies on Germany.

Germany and the Germans in the early nineteenth century

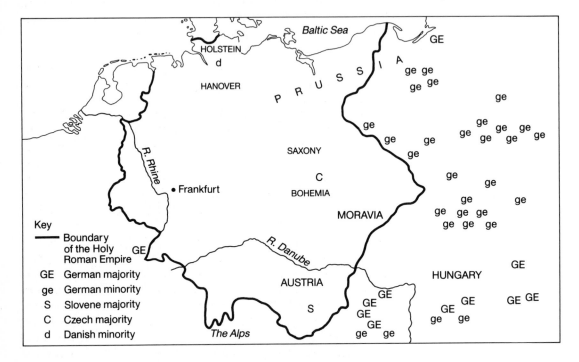

Fig 1.2   The Holy Roman Empire in the late eighteenth century.

In 1800 Germany presented, as it had done for centuries, a confusing picture of large and small states, set within the frame of the Holy Roman Empire. The Holy Roman Emperor claimed to be the direct successor of the rulers of Ancient Rome. In theory he was the overlord of an empire which stretched from the Rhine in the west to the Danube in the east, and from the Baltic in the north to the Alps in the south. (Refer to Figure 1.2 for the boundaries of the Holy Roman Empire and for the other places mentioned in this section.) In fact his only real power was as the ruler of the Habsburg Empire, parts of which were in the Holy Roman Empire (Austria, Bohemia and Moravia) and parts of which were outside it (notably Hungary). The other parts of the Holy Roman Empire were in practice independent.

Apart from the Habsburg Empire, only one part of the Holy Roman Empire was a large and important state – the kingdom of Prussia, which stretched across what is now north Germany. Many of the other states were extremely small. There were almost 400 of them. Some were city states, like Frankfurt. Some were ruled by the Catholic church – either by the local bishop (who was called a Prince Bishop if he ruled a state), or by the local monastery or abbey (which was called an Imperial Abbey if it ruled even the tiniest state in the Holy Roman Empire). Some were small pieces of countryside ruled by the local landowner (who because of this was called an Imperial Knight). A few were medium-sized states like Hanover and Saxony; the rulers of these were called Electors, because in theory they elected the Holy Roman Emperor (although in practice he was always the Habsburg Emperor).

As if this were not confusing enough, not everyone in the Holy Roman Empire was German. You will see from Figure 1.2 that many people in Holstein were Danes, and most people in Bohemia were Czechs. And to make it even more confusing, not all the Germans lived in the Holy Roman Empire. This was partly because active and enterprising German families had over the centuries made better lives for themselves by settling in different parts of eastern Europe, and they had come to be important minorities in these places – for example, in Estonia, Lithuania, Poland, Galicia, Hungary, and parts of Russia. However, it is difficult to understand why East Prussia, which was mainly inhabited by Germans, was outside the Holy Roman Empire.

It was, therefore, almost impossible to say in the early 1800s exactly what or where Germany was. However, the Germans obviously had their own language and culture, and indeed their writers, thinkers and artists were the most famous in Europe at that time. They included the composer Beethoven, the playwright Schiller, the philosopher and teacher Hegel, and, most famous of all at the time, the poet and writer Goethe. The collectors of ancient folk-tales whom you read about on page 12 were part of the same great flowering of German culture. These men were certainly not all German nationalists. Goethe was not greatly interested in politics, and he continued to admire Napoleon till his final defeat. What these great intellectuals did, however, was to win for Germans the position of cultural leaders of Europe – a position which for over a century before had been held by the French. It is ironic that at this very time French armies were conquering large parts of Germany. In doing this Napoleon quite unintentionally laid some of the foundations for the eventual unification of Germany.

Napoleon and Germany

From 1792 the lands in the Holy Roman Empire west of the River Rhine became part of France. This gave Germans who cared about such things (then a small minority) an early indication that revolutionary France was not likely to give to other nations the rights that it had promised.

It was, however, Napoleon who carried out major changes in Germany. The most important of these came after he had decisively beaten Austria in 1805 at the battles of Ulm and Austerlitz, and Prussia in 1806 at Jena and Auerstadt. The two leading German states were humiliated and lost large territories, but they were at least allowed to survive as separate states. The more fundamental and lasting changes which Napoleon made were in the rest of Germany, which he was now free to rearrange as he wished. His orderly, modern mind and his need to have reliable client states on France's eastern frontier both suggested to him that the ancient patchwork of the Holy Roman Empire must go. He described the Holy Roman Empire as 'a miserable monkey house' and dissolved it in August 1806.

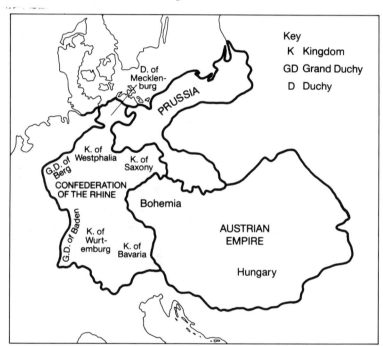

Fig 1.3
Germany in 1806.

Napoleon redrew the map of Germany (see Figure 1.3). The nearly 400 states of the Holy Roman Empire were reduced in number to thirty-nine. Apart from the Habsburg lands (now called the Austrian Empire) and Prussia, most of these states were grouped in the 'Confederation of the Rhine', which was under French control. One of these, the kingdom of Westphalia, was actually given a French ruler (Napoleon's brother Jerome). Other new states were ruled (within limits laid down by Napoleon) by princes from some of the old states which had been forcibly merged. The princes were reconciled to this by being elevated to royal rank. At a stroke Napoleon created the kingdoms of Saxony, Hanover, Bavaria and Württemberg. These four were the most important of the 'Middle States', whose purpose was to act as a buffer between France and her potential enemies to the east – Austria, Prussia and Russia. The Middle States were middling also in size – big enough (unlike their predecessors) to provide reasonable protection for France, but not big enough to ignore French wishes.

In Figure 1.4 you will see Napoleon formally inaugurating the Confederation of the Rhine in 1806. As the rulers of the Middle States stand to salute him, he brandishes a sword, thus demonstrating in a very direct and frank way the basis of his power over Germany.

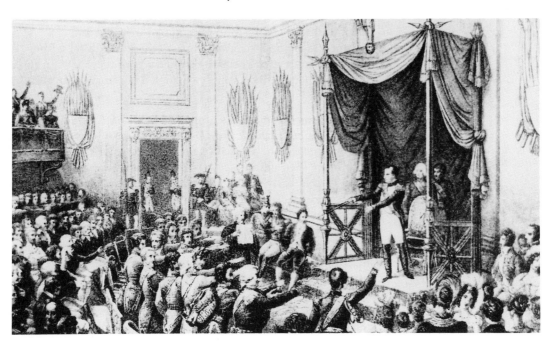

Fig 1.4 Napoleon inaugurating the Confederation of the Rhine in 1806.

Many people in Germany were not outraged by this. For example, Goethe wrote in his diary for 6 and 7 August 1806:

'Seven o'clock in the evening at Hof. Announcement of the proclamation of the Confederation of the Rhine. Good dinner. Quarrel between servant and coachman which excited us more than the dissolution of the Roman Empire.'

The rulers of the Middle States were given considerable freedom in the ways in which they carried out French policies, provided that they kept to the overall programme laid down by Napoleon. Thus Saxony, Bavaria, and the others worked out their own ways of reducing the powers of the landowners, placing the church and the schools under state control, and adopting a legal system based on the new French 'Code Napoleon'. In any case, many of their subjects approved of these French imports, and were pleased to see some of them survive when Napoleon went. However, there was always something improbable and temporary in a situation in which Napoleon, the leader of revolutionary France, presented himself as the real successor of the Holy Roman Emperors of old, and in which he created and controlled kingdoms in the Confederation of the Rhine. As Golo Mann puts it:

> 'Napoleon, always anxious to cloak his rootless power with the magic of age, vainly used various institutions and ceremonies to stress this continuity. How in the long run could Germany allow itself to be ruled from Paris? How could post-revolutionary, middle class Europe believe in Charlemagne's imperial mantle which a foreign general, a product of the Revolution, claimed to be wearing? The great realist was also a great dreamer. He mistook passing opportunities and advantages for final achievements, confused the tinsel with which he covered the craziest by-products of the war with real gold, and became increasingly entangled in romantic dreams.'
>
> (*The History of Germany Since 1789*)

Throughout Napoleon's Europe, there was a contradiction between the rights that the Emperor gave to people as individuals and the rights that he refused to give to nations so that they could control their own destinies.

During the early 1800s an increasing number of Germans (mainly middle class merchants, officials and teachers) came to resent French domination. Whether they were Prussians who resented the way in which they had been humiliated on the battlefield, or Bavarians who resented the way in which their king danced to the French tune, they wanted Germans to have more control over their own affairs. And this feeling was encouraged by the increasing interest in Germany's past. All these different threads can be seen coming together in the *Addresses to the German Nation* given in 1807 and 1808 by Fichte, the Rector of Berlin University:

> '[For the early Germans who fought against the Roman legions] liberty to them meant this: persisting to remain German and continuing the task of settling their own problems, independently... They assumed as a matter of course that every German would rather die than become Roman... We, the inheritors of their soil, their language and their way of thinking, must thank them for being Germans.
>
> Our present problem... is simply to preserve the existence and continuity of what is German. All other differences vanish before this higher point of view... It is essential that the higher love of Fatherland, for the entire people of the German nation, reigns supreme, and justly so, in every particular German state.'

Here Fichte is telling the Germans of his own day that they should fight the French invaders in the way that their ancestors fought the Romans.

In the early 1800s nationalists like Fichte were still a small minority among Germans. However, Napoleon's treatment of Germany was increasing their number year by year. By greatly reducing the number of German states, Napoleon had also ensured that Germany could eventually be united much more easily than it otherwise could have been.

The 1815 settlement and Germany
The 'War of Liberation'

The final defeat of Napoleon was described by Germans in later years as the 'War of Liberation'. However, Germans did not play the leading part in this war. The Russian winter played a major part, as Napoleon lost 350,000 men on his retreat from Moscow at the end of his disastrous invasion in 1812. The Russian Emperor, Alexander I, also played a major part when he resolved to pursue Napoleon all the way to Paris. And the British played a major part by being the only power to stand against Napoleon throughout the years from 1805 onwards.

Of the Germans, the Prussians had the most reason to congratulate themselves on winning a 'War of Liberation'. After their humiliation at the battles of Jena and Auerstadt in 1806, they had reformed their state (under Stein and Hardenburg) and rebuilt their army (under Scharnhorst and Gneisenau). They had paid the French the compliment of copying their methods. As Hardenburg put it to the king of Prussia, 'We must do from above what the French have done from below.' As a result, the peasants were freed from being the property of the landowners. Schools and universities were reformed, and this improved the quality of education. The generals built up a mass army on the French pattern. The new army enabled King Frederick William III of Prussia to make an alliance with Russia in January 1813 (six months before Austria came back into the war). Prussian soldiers sang new patriotic songs as they marched to share in the decisive victory at Leipzig in October 1813 and in the wintry march across the Rhine which followed it.

In contrast, the Middle States of Germany were only persuaded to abandon Napoleon when it became clear that his cause was lost. Figure 1.5 shows Napoleon's rise and fall as seen by a German cartoonist in 1814. You will see that, after his retreat from Moscow, it is commanders of the major powers who are shown driving him out of Germany.

Golo Mann argues that the Germans were left with a feeling of shame for the relatively inactive part that they had played during

Fig 1.5   *The rise and fall of Napoleon, as seen by a German artist in 1814.*

the French Revolutionary and Napoleonic Wars, and that this feeling was to be very important later:

'Things happened to Germany, but they were done to it by others. The country adapted itself... but it was only a process of adaptation, voluntary or compulsory, to great events elsewhere. The French Revolution was hot, the German cold... There were no public meetings, no storming of Bastilles and no guillotines. The storm blew elsewhere, Germany only felt its effects. As a result the Germans had in years to come no wish to look back and be proud of the great political and social transformation that occurred at the beginning of the nineteenth century; they saw it as a time of shame. The Germans became active – against France – only during the last act of the long revolutionary drama, in 1813. Even then they did not play a really glorious role comparable with that of the British or the Russians. Though the "War of Liberation" was a notable effort on the part of the Germans, it was not the popular uprising that contemporary, and even more, later imagination wanted to make of it.

It was not in 1813–14 that Germany took revenge for its passivity during the Napoleonic drama. The real reaction to that experience came later, in the second half of the century. What psychologists teach about the individual also applies to the nation: it can harbour old, unpleasant memories, transform them in strange ways and derive aggressive energies from them.'

(*The History of Germany Since 1789*)

ESSAY

Choose one of the following views about the origins of German nationalism to 1815, and write an essay to discuss it.

1. 'Nationalism in Germany owed more to the French Revolution than to German culture and traditions.'

2. 'Napoleon did more than he knew for the cause of German nationalism.'

3. 'The events of 1789–1815 showed there was little prospect of Germany being united.'

The growth of German nationalism, 1815–60

When the Emperor Napoleon was finally defeated at the Battle of Waterloo in June 1815, it seemed to bring to an end a period of great excitement in Europe. For twenty-five years the ideas of the French Revolution and the might of French armies had thrust themselves into almost every part of Europe and had upset the old ways of doing things. This was particularly true of Germany, where much of the fighting had taken place and where many of the little states into which Germany had been divided had disappeared. After 1815, the excitement seemed to be over. Many of the old ways were restored. Otto von Bismarck, who played a greater part than any other individual in eventually bringing Germany together as one state, described the years after 1815 as 'the time when nothing happened'.

The German states may have remained separate at this time but, if we look under the surface, we can see that Germany was gradually changing. We can find out why it was changing by thinking about several issues:

1. How great after 1815 were the prospects of the different states of Germany being united?
2. What changes were brought about in Germany by the growth of industry and large towns, and why did these changes encourage the growth of nationalism?
3. Why did the 1848 revolutions fail to bring about German unification?
4. How had the relative power of the Austrian Empire and Prussia changed by 1860?

These issues raise questions about the sense of *identity* of German people, the *authority* of the existing German states, and the *ideology* of different groups of people in Germany.

TASK

Work in pairs.

Some students will look for evidence in this chapter to support Bismarck's view that the period from 1815 to the 1850s was 'the time when nothing happened' to move Germany towards unification.

Others will look for evidence in the chapter which suggests that in this period German nationalism was growing, and that the chances of Germany being united were increasing.

Note and organise the evidence.

Then hold a debate on the motion that 'By 1860 nothing really important had happened to move Germany towards unification.'

Make notes on the evidence produced by those arguing the opposite case.

The 1815 settlement

It was no surprise that a united Germany was not created in the peace settlement of 1815. It had not been a united country since the Middle Ages and only a relatively few Germans wanted it to be united now. Some Prussian officials and officers may have wanted it, but their king most certainly did not. The rulers of the other German states did not want it. They wanted to keep control of their own little parts of Germany.

One of the principles on which the victorious powers based the settlement was 'the restoration of legitimacy'. This meant that, where practicable, hereditary rulers would be given back their lands. In theory this implied, not merely that there would be no united Germany, but also that there should have been a return to the nearly 400 states of the Holy Roman Empire. This was rejected by the victors because another principle was seen as being even more important – that of ensuring a balance of power in Europe.

Representatives of all the rulers of Europe met in Vienna in 1814 and 1815 to make a peace settlement, and continued their work through the 'One hundred days' in the early summer of 1815 when Napoleon returned from exile to make a final, doomed attempt to rescue his empire. It was a glittering show. Representatives were lodged in the various palaces of Vienna and balls were put on practically every evening to entertain them. The most influential figures in the serious meetings were Prince Metternich (representing the Austrian Empire) and Lord Castlereagh (representing Great Britain). Prussia had done more than the Austrian Empire to defeat Napoleon (not least in the final battle at Waterloo in June 1815), but had no statesman of the diplomatic skill of Metternich.

Castlereagh and Metternich saw the most likely threats to the future peace of Europe as coming from France (because of her record over the previous twenty years), or from Russia (because she had alarmed the other powers in 1813 and 1814 by showing that her army was capable of marching right across Europe and because her emperor, Alexander I, was liable to produce grandiose schemes). If either France or Russia were to try to expand, it was likely to be into Germany, which must therefore be made secure. It could not be secure if hundreds of tiny states were restored. Nor could it could be united because that would encourage nationalist movements in Italy, Hungary and throughout the Austrian Empire. None of the major powers believed that the collapse of the Austrian Empire would help to keep the peace of Europe (and Metternich was determined to prevent this).

To have a balance of power in Europe, there must be a balance of power in Germany. Thus Prussia and Austria were given extra territories, so that they would be powerful enough to defend Germany, but would keep each other in check. And so that neither would become too powerful, the other German states would be left more or less as they had been arranged by Napoleon.

The settlement of Germany was made in the Treaty of Vienna and the German Act of Confederation, adopted within days of one another in June 1815. Figure 2.1 shows the arrangement of the separate German states which was to survive until 1866. You will see that, as a gesture towards restoring the old order, the boundary of the new German Confederation was almost the same as that of the Holy Roman Empire (as shown in Figure 1.2), which Napoleon had dissolved in 1806. But the states within the confederation were the same thirty-nine that Napoleon had arranged – with some adjustment of boundaries for the benefit of those who had contributed most to his downfall. Not only the Great Powers, but also the rulers of the German states were pleased that this meant that the confederation would be difficult to make into a united Germany. The rulers did not want it to develop in that way.

The way in which the confederation worked was also designed to make it difficult for it to develop into a united Germany. These extracts from the Act of Confederation show that each state was given so much power that it would be almost impossible for the confederation to become a united Germany:

'The sovereign princes and the free towns of Germany . . . convinced of the advantages which would accrue for the security and independence of Germany and for the well-being and equilibrium of Europe from a strong and lasting union, have agreed to unite themselves in a perpetual confederation.

Article 1: The sovereign princes and the free towns of Germany, including their Majesties, the Emperor of Austria and the Kings of Prussia and Denmark . . . unite in a perpetual union which shall be called the German Confederation.

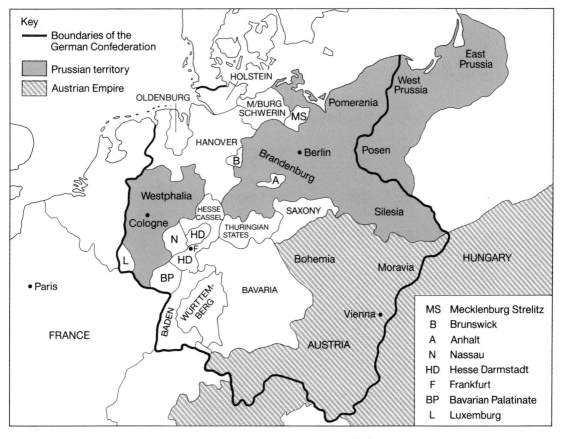

Fig 2.1   The German Confederation, 1815–66.

Article 2: The aim of this confederation shall be the maintenance of the external and internal security of Germany as well as the independence of the individual German states.

Article 3: All members of the Confederation shall have equal rights.

Article 4: The affairs of the Confederation shall be managed by a Federal Assembly in which all members of the Confederation shall be represented by their ambassadors, who shall each have one vote.'

How fiercely the rulers of the individual states guarded their independence is shown by the fact that the confederation was not even able to carry out some of the common functions which had been agreed on in the Act which set it up. They did nothing to agree on a policy to make it easier to trade between the states. Although they eventually (after six years) agreed to set up a federal army, the states would not give up their control over their contingents in the army – which made the army almost unworkable. William Carr has explained why Metternich did not want the German states to co-operate too closely:

> 'Balance was the key to Metternich's "system". He was firmly convinced that monarchs could sit securely on their thrones only when the balance of forces inside society favoured the established order, and when the balance of power between states was strong enough to deter potential aggressors... He had no doubt that the success of demands for freedom in Germany and Italy would lead inevitably to the destruction of the precarious foundations of Habsburg power, and the disruption of the European balance of power... To keep the dark forces at bay in Central Europe, Metternich relied on the prestige of Austria and on the goodwill and co-operation of the German princes... In the interests of European peace the princes would have to relinquish the right to wage war on each other and agree to live together in a loose association or confederation of states. At the same time the fact that the princes would remain rulers of virtually sovereign states was the best possible insurance against the creation of a united Germany.'
>
> *(A History of Germany 1815–1945)*

Germany and German nationalism, 1815–48
Cultural nationalism

We have seen that some Germans had become nationalists by 1815. Humiliated by the way in which Napoleon had treated Germany, and enthused by speeches like those of Fichte and by the folk-tales collected by the Grimm brothers and others, they looked back on Germany's past with pride and longed for the day when Germany would be a united and independent nation. This may be called 'cultural nationalism', because it owed so much to a love of Germany's culture and history. However, it did not seem very likely in the years after 1815 that this would succeed in uniting Germany. It is true that support for this form of nationalism was increased by resentment at what Napoleon had done to Germany and then by enthusiasm aroused by the War of Liberation. But there were many reasons which made it seem likely in 1815 that the German states would stay apart.

We have seen that the constitution of the new German Confederation was designed to make it difficult for it to develop into a united state. There was great rivalry between Prussia and Austria for control of Germany. Both had been strengthened by the 1815 settlement. Austria had been strengthened by major gains outside Germany (mainly in Italy) and by the important part that her foreign minister, Metternich, had played in framing the settlement. Prussia's gains in north Germany meant that she dominated that part of the country. It seemed unlikely that either would give way to the other. The fact that more of the Austrian lands were non-German made it even more difficult for one of the rivals simply to win the struggle and to take over the rest of Germany.

Unification was also likely to be delayed by the fact that nationalist feelings were much stronger in Prussia than in the Middle States, which had mostly fitted in with Napoleon's requirements without too much unhappiness. This division between Prussia and the Middle States was reinforced by a religious gulf almost 300 years old. The Middle States (and Prussia's new lands by the Rhine) were mostly Catholic, whereas the older Prussian dominions in north Germany were firmly Protestant.

But even in Prussia, where nationalism was strongest, it was not *German* nationalism which principally inspired the most important class of people. The loyalty of the junkers (or landowners) was to the *Prussian* state and to the *Prussian* king. It was they who had helped the Hohenzollern monarchs to take Prussia in a little over a century from being a modest state in the far north-east of Germany to being one of the great powers of Europe. They were proud of their achievement and wanted to preserve it. Furthermore, the junkers had come through the trauma of defeat by Napoleon in 1806 with their authority almost as great as ever. In theory the peasants were now allowed to go where they wished and work for whoever they wanted. However, there was little land for them and they still depended on the junkers for work as farm labourers. As the junkers also kept control of local courts, it was still they who ran the Prussian countryside (where more than 90 per cent of the population lived in 1815). The junkers also kept control of the Prussian army, which was now larger and more powerful than ever. Although other classes were now allowed to become officers, most of them were still in fact junkers. The firm loyalty of most of the junkers to Prussia was, therefore, a real barrier to German unification.

Despite these obstacles, the authorities in all the German states were concerned about nationalism, and after 1815 they thought that the main threat came from writers and thinkers and from the university students who were influenced by them. Some of the writing of this period was very pro-German and very anti-French (because of what Napoleon had done to Germany). This can be seen in a poem by Ernst Arndt called 'The German Fatherland':

'What is the fatherland of the German? Name me the great country! Where the German tongue sounds and sings German songs in God's praise, that's where it ought to be . . . This is the Fatherland of the German where anger roots out foreign nonsense, where every Frenchman is called enemy, where every German is called friend.'

Arndt calls here for a Germany which would cover a very wide area indeed. Friedrich Jahn had similar hopes, and he was determined to do something practical to bring them about. He saw education as the key to uniting Germany. Jahn believed that Germans must be tougher if they were to fight for unity, and he set up schools in which boys followed a programme of gymnastic exercises designed to make them strong and self-confident. When they passed on to university, Jahn did not want them to waste their time in the traditional student societies, dedicated to drinking, duelling and pursuing women. He set up the new 'Burschenshaften' students' movement. It aimed to reform the morals of students and to develop in them an interest in politics. The views of these nationalist students are summed up in a speech made by one of them, Karl von Hase, at Leipzig in 1820:

'A people who fought seven years ago on this battlefield is worthy of a better fate. And if the magnificence of the great day has disappeared, if all the palms of victory have withered, if all the medals and trophies of great victories have faded, one thing remains and shall remain, that is the vision proclaimed on that day . . .

The first vision seems to me to be this: happiness and leisure are not the highest aims of the people, but freedom . . .

From this it follows: the happiness and the greatness of a people depend only on the highest possible liberty of all citizens and the equality of all, established by laws they make themselves or that are made by their representatives.

The third . . . an enthusiastic people which is willing to fight for such laws and for such a Fatherland cannot be conquered . . .

The fourth belongs to us alone and is the most beautiful of all: Germans are we all together . . . made equal through speech, customs and descent, all citizens of Germany – a unified people of brothers is irresistible.'

For the authorities in most German states these were very alarming views because they combined nationalism with liberalism.

Liberalism was the view that a state should not be governed by a monarch and his servants without any real means for ordinary people to question their actions (as was the case in most German states at this time). There should be freedom to write and speak freely, and to form political parties; and the wealthier and better educated members of the population should have a say in politics by voting on how the country was governed.

Since Germany could not be united until the control of the

rulers of the individual states was broken, most nationalists were also liberal. The authorities were very nervous of the students who held views which seemed to be a double threat for them. They were very alarmed when in 1817 500 students met at Wartburg Castle to celebrate the three-hundredth anniversary of the Reformation and the fourth anniversary of Napoleon's defeat at the Battle of Leipzig (which showed that this form of German nationalism was Protestant and anti-French). At the end of the formal celebrations, some of Jahn's supporters from Berlin burnt books opposed to their views – which does not seem to be a very liberal action! Figure 2.2 shows them doing this (with the castle in the background).

Fig 2.2 German students burn anti-patriotic books in Wartburg in 1817.

It was because the authorities were so alarmed by the unrest among students that they reacted so strongly when in 1819 a student (who was mentally unbalanced) murdered Kotzebue, a secret agent and an anti-liberal writer. Metternich thought that the students threatened the 1815 settlement of Germany. He called together representatives of the German states and they issued the 'Carlsbad Decrees' which disbanded student societies; ordered the appointment of inspectors to keep order in universities; and introduced censorship of newspapers.

It seems clear now that Metternich overreacted and that the students were a limited group of talkers and dreamers with no real plan of action. However, the Carlsbad Decrees certainly succeeded in keeping Germany quiet for a considerable period of time.

It was not until the 1830s that there was much more nationalist agitation. In 1832, 25,000 nationalists met at the Hambach Festival in Bavaria. A new students' movement called 'Young Germany' appeared, and in 1833 a hopeless armed rising by students took place.

Most historians now believe that liberal and nationalist views did not spread very widely through Germany in the first half of the nineteenth century. It seems that these ideas were held by relatively limited numbers of educated town-dwellers, who wrote and talked, but who had no clear idea of what action should be taken. Some of them tried to get the support of groups of town workers, but they never seem to have held their interest for long.

There may not have been many active nationalists at this period. But an incident in 1840 showed that nationalism was now close to the surface of German life and could be whipped up very quickly if Germany seemed to be threatened. In that year France was trying to get the agreement of the other European powers that she should be allowed to control Egypt. As a bargaining counter, the French threatened to extend their eastern frontier (as they had done in 1792) to the Rhine. They claimed that the Rhine was their natural frontier. There was an uproar throughout Germany – not merely in the parts of the Rhineland which would be affected; not merely in Prussia, whose territory it now was; and not merely among the middle class enthusiasts of nationalism. In a way which had not happened even during the War of Liberation, large numbers of ordinary Germans were outraged, and they expressed their determination to defend the Fatherland in popular songs: 'Like thunder rolls the cry, to the Rhine, to the German, German Rhine.' Figure 2.3 shows a German cartoon based on another of the songs of 1840: 'They shall never have the old German Rhine.'

The events of 1840 show that by now nationalism had had some impact on people throughout Germany, even if they did not show it very often. It was also important for the future that, as it was her territory which was threatened, it was Prussia which got the credit for keeping 'The Watch on the Rhine' (– this was the title of another of the popular songs of 1840).

Frankreich.

Singt nicht zu laut, zum Zeitvertreibe,
Die Lungen Euch aus deutschem Leibe,
Sonst machen wir, mit Bomben und Kanonen,
Auf Euer Lied, die Variationen.

Deutschland.

Lärmt, wie Ihr wollt, Ihr links am Rheine,
Nur werft herüber nicht mit Blei,
Sonst schlagen wir Euch Arm' und Beine,
Und Kreuz und Schädel morsch entzwei.

Fig 2.3   Cartoon illustrating the Rhine crisis in 1840.

Economic nationalism

Some historians argue that the really important changes in nineteenth-century Europe were not brought about by ideas (cultural nationalism), but by social and economic developments. The population of Europe, which in previous centuries had remained static or had grown very slowly, increased nearly four-fold in the 200 years after 1750. One historian, David Thomson, claims that:

> 'No social and political order could have remained unaffected by so immense an increase of humanity. And the events of the nineteenth century remain unintelligible unless the greatest revolution of all is kept constantly in mind.'

This population explosion was accompanied by the growth of industry and by the accelerating movement of people from the countryside to the towns to take up new jobs in factories and warehouses. In these developments Britain was first off the mark and remained ahead of other European countries for most of the nineteenth century. The German historian Golo Mann has written:

> 'What finally led the "people" to active participation in politics was the slow irresistible change in society. It has been said that it is impossible to fight ideas, but while they are only ideas they can be fought. Rulers who try to avoid changes in the way countries are run are powerless against the hidden and automatic social progress which, day by day, year by year, transforms small towns into cities and craftsmen into employers and employed. So it happened that a political system which in 1816 was reasonably suited to the way people lived lost more and more of its usefulness until in the middle of the century there was great unrest. A steady drip, not a cloudburst, wears down the stone. From the stage-coach to the railway, the steamship and the telegraph, this is a story of tremendous change in the way people lived and thought.'
>
> (*The History of Germany Since 1789*)

We will now consider how much these social and economic changes contributed to the growth of nationalism and to moves towards the unification of Germany in the first half of the nineteenth century.

It is certainly true that the population of Germany rose from almost 25 million in 1816 to over 34 million in 1845. In 1815 only 10 per cent of Germans lived in towns. Industrialists did not own large factories, but had small workshops staffed by skilled workmen, or, in many cases, had work done in the homes of people in the surrounding countryside. By the 1840s, some towns were growing fast (for example, the number of people in Berlin grew by 100,000 in the 1840s), and large cotton mills and iron and engineering works were beginning to appear.

It has been suggested that these developments pushed Germany towards unification in several ways:

Customs union

In 1815 the German states had their own currencies, their own systems of weights and measures, and their own laws on trade. Goods being transported across Germany were liable to customs duties every time they crossed into another state. These arrangements had to be rationalised if German trade was to expand. A start was made in 1818, when Prussia decided to set up her own customs union by abolishing the many customs barriers within her territories. A low rate of tax would be charged on goods which were being imported to be sold in Prussia; but a high rate would be charged on goods which were passing through to other states. As Prussian territories dominated northern Germany, this was very inconvenient to other states – not only to those in the north, but also to those in the centre and south – which wished to trade along the great rivers controlled by Prussia, such as the Rhine and the Elbe. First some of the smaller states joined the Prussian customs union. Then in 1834 it became the 'Zollverein', when Bavaria and Württemberg joined it. By 1836 it included twenty-five of the thirty-nine states, all of which had to accept Prussian control of the machinery to collect the customs dues and Prussian trade law.

Metternich had objected strongly to the Zollverein when it was set up:

> 'Now a number of independent states accept, in relation to a neighbour superior in power, the obligation of conforming to its laws and its controls in a most important branch of public finance... Little by little, under the direction of Prussia and because of common interests, the states which make up this union will compose a more or less compact body, acting in common.'

It seems clear that one of Prussia's principal aims in setting up the Zollverein and the other states' main reasons for joining it and remaining in it were to build up their trade and wealth. This can be seen from the reasons Württemberg officials give here for advising in the early 1850s that they should stay in the Zollverein and not enter a new customs union with Austria:

> 'Württemberg's trade routes go in the main towards the North Sea... a breach of the trade links with Prussia, who rules the Rhine for a long stretch on both banks, would cause the most damaging disturbance of trade... during the eighteen years that the Zollverein has existed, contacts in trade have become so many and the interests of the businessmen have so interlocked with each other that the tearing apart of these countries would be accompanied by the most damaging effect upon industry and trade.'

However, Prussia had more reasons than just the economic ones for setting up the Zollverein. She certainly saw it as a way of uniting her own territories. She probably saw it as a way of isolating Austria. She may have seen it, as was later claimed, as 'the mighty lever of German unification'. Individual Prussians hinted at this. For example, the finance minister said in the 1830s that 'unification of these states in a customs and trading union leads to the establishment of a unified political system'.

Some historians have argued that, if the Prussians did hope for this, it just did not happen. The other states in the Zollverein regularly went against Prussian wishes in political matters. Other historians say that, unless they felt strongly about something, the Zollverein states would tend to follow Prussia because their trade links with her were so profitable. For example, William Carr comments:

> 'Certainly Prussia was not thinking in terms of political unification when she founded the Customs Union. Nor had the states joined it out of love for Prussia but simply and solely to escape from the financial and economic difficulties which beset them. Political rivalries were not in any way diminished by the success of the Customs Union; the members continued to eye Prussia with suspicion and they guarded their own independence jealously even in purely commercial matters.
>
> All the same, the Customs Union was an object lesson for the German people. Eighteen states had voluntarily restricted their sovereignty in the common interest, an action without precedent in the history of the Confederation. This was a first step towards a wider political union.'
>
> (*A History of Germany 1815–1945*)

Pressure from businessmen

By the 1840s there had been a reduction in the number of different systems of customs, weights and measures, and of different systems of commercial law. Nevertheless German businessmen still felt that they could not compete on equal terms with Britain until Germany was united. It was not for purely cultural reasons that nationalism was strongest among middle class townspeople at this time. The business reasons were publicised for many years by Friedrich List. This extract from a book published in 1841 is typical of his arguments in favour of unification:

> 'I saw clearly that free competition between two nations which are highly civilised can be mutually beneficial only where both of them are in a nearly equal position of industrial development, and that any nation which . . . is getting behind others . . . must first of all strengthen its own individual powers . . . I felt that Germany must abolish her internal customs duties . . . The German nation cannot be complete as long as it does not extend over the whole coast from the mouth of the Rhine to the frontier of Poland.'

Pressure from workers

Dissatisfied industrial workers wanted to change the way in which they were ruled. As in Britain, some of the workers who had moved from the countryside to get jobs in factories found it difficult to make a living or to find decent accommodation in the crowded towns. A particular problem in Germany was posed by craftsmen, who now had to compete with the new factories, and found themselves either without work or having to accept much reduced wages. As we shall see, economic depression did much to bring about the revolutions of 1848. In Germany discontented craftsmen played a particularly important part, and for a brief period in 1848 and 1849 it looked as if Germany might be united.

It can be argued, therefore, that economic and social developments were undermining the German states and pushing Germany towards unification.

How powerful these economic and social forces were by 1848 can be worked out from this table, which shows how German industry had grown, in comparison with British industry:

	Coal production		Pig iron production	
	Annual average (in million tonnes)		Annual average (in thousand tonnes)	
	Germany	UK	Germany	UK
Late 1820s	1.6	22.3	90	669
Late 1830s	3.0	28.1	146	1142
Late 1840s	6.1	48.6	184	1786

You will see that German industry was growing in the 1830s and 1840s, but it was still very small in comparison with British industry. Businessmen were not yet such a powerful group in German life as they were to become later: of Germany's population of over 34 milion in the late 1840s, only about 600,000 were industrial workers.

The 1848 revolutions showed up in fact the weaknesses of economic, social and cultural pressures for German unification at that time.

The 1848 revolutions

1848 has been called 'The Year of Revolutions'. The first revolution was at the end of February, when King Louis-Philippe fled from Paris and a French Republic was proclaimed. This was the spark which lit the fire of revolution across Europe. It was not only the desire for liberty which persuaded the peoples of Europe to demonstrate and fight against their rulers, but also the demand for bread. The last few years had seen bad harvests throughout Europe. In Germany, as elsewhere, peasants had had great difficulty in feeding their families, and some had moved to the towns to look for work. But there was no salvation for them there.

There had been an economic recession across Europe since 1846. Orders for industrial goods became harder to win; factories closed down, and little was done to help the workers who became unemployed.

In late February and in March mass meetings and petitions persuaded rulers throughout Germany to agree to such demands as freedom of the press and control of the government by an elected parliament (as in Britain). The most spectacular example was in the Austrian Empire. The Austrian Chancellor Metternich (who had been the most powerful figure in Germany for thirty years) fled from Vienna to London. The non-German peoples of the empire (such as the Hungarians and the Italians) pressed for greater independence.

In many of these upheavals there was at first no serious violence, but in Prussia a demonstration of craftsmen outside the royal palace in Berlin sparked off several days of street fighting. The ferocity of the fighting there can be seen in Figure 2.4, which shows a battle between soldiers and demonstrators outside the royal palace, and in this account:

'Everywhere students, citizens and working men rushed into the streets, supplied themselves with weapons, ammunition, axes and iron bars and rushed to the barricades, which in some streets reached to the first floor windows. By seven o'clock most of the Konigstrasse had been taken by the soldiers – the whole street swam with blood.'

Fig 2.4   The 1848 revolution in Berlin – fighting in front of the royal palace.

Fig 2.5 The dead are carried before the king and queen.

King Frederick William IV was now humiliated by the revolutionaries, as shown in Figure 2.5 and in the report which accompanied it in *The Illustrated London News*:

'In the early morning several waggons were filled with the slain corpses and wounded bodies of the citizens of Berlin, which were carried in funeral procession to the courtyard of the palace. The King was loudly called for; he appeared on the balcony, was requested to descend to the courtyard and, uncovered, to survey the fearful spectacle. Cries were raised for the Queen; and on his Majesty affirming that she was so alarmed as to be in an unfit state to appear, the cries were more loudly repeated; the King thereupon retired and shortly afterwards returned, leading the Queen by the hand. They were dreadfully affected at the awful scene, which they gazed on for a few moments in solemn silence; after which the crowd peaceably dispersed, carrying with them the torn and bleeding remains of their friends and neighbours.'

When the killing of 300 rioters by troops failed to halt the troubles, King Frederick William seemed to put himself at the head of the revolution by wearing the German colours (black, red and gold), by announcing that he was in favour of liberty and of a united Germany, and by offering to lead the struggle for unification. The turmoil within the Austrian Empire meant that he might have a chance of uniting Germany. He issued this proclamation:

> 'To my people and to the German nation – Germany is in a state of internal ferment and can be threatened by external danger from more than one side. It can be saved from this double danger only by the most intimate unity of the German princes and peoples under one leadership. Today I take over this leadership for the days of danger . . . I have today taken the old German colours . . . Prussia henceforth merges into Germany.'

In this proclamation he also promised to co-operate with the German parliament which was to meet in Frankfurt in May. The German rulers agreed to the parliament being elected because they were afraid that they would lose their thrones if they did not show themselves willing to consider changes in the way Germany was governed.

The Frankfurt parliament was elected in such a way that most of its members were middle class and well-educated. Most of them were liberal and nationalist. They wanted a united Germany under a monarch who would rule through a parliament elected by well-to-do and well-educated citizens (in other words, by people like themselves). However, this would take time to work out, and meantime the parliament appointed a provisional government which would act through the existing states.

The weakness of this was soon shown. At first Prussia carried out instructions from the parliament to drive the Danes out of the duchies of Schleswig and Holstein in order to make them part of Germany. But she then changed her mind, made an armistice agreement with Denmark and withdrew her troops from the duchies. For by this time King Fredrick William IV had decided that he did not want to unite Germany with the help of revolutionaries.

Nationalists throughout Germany were outraged. However, the parliament decided that it must accept the Prussian decision. It believed that it might need Prussian troops to put down the disturbances by workers and peasants which were now taking place in various parts of Germany. For example, machines, railways and steamships were being wrecked by hungry people who blamed them for making them unemployed. This was a threat not only to the traditional rulers, but also to the middle class liberals who dominated the Frankfurt parliament. Many of the owners of the factories and the new transport undertakings were middle class liberals.

How much the parliament depended on the existing states was shown in September, shortly after it agreed to the Prussian armistice with Denmark. Prussian and Austrian troops had to be called in to defend the parliament against an armed attack by people who thought that it had betrayed the German cause. These events were a serious blow to the parliament's prestige.

As 1848 wore on into 1849, the parliament was unable to work out any precise plan as to how Germany should be governed. Meantime, the tide of revolution was receding across Europe. The Austrian government gradually restored its authority in its various territories. In March 1849 the new emperor, Francis Joseph, was able formally to restore complete control of the empire from Vienna. This was incompatible with Austria becoming part of a united and liberal Germany. It was only now that the German parliament was able to decide that the king of Prussia should be invited to become emperor of Germany and to finalise the constitution under which he would rule. By this time Frederick William had restored his power in Prussia. He now had no intention of encouraging revolutionaries and his reaction to the parliament's invitation was, therefore, very different from what he had said in his proclamation in March 1848:

> 'Privately he said that "Every German nobleman is a hundred times too good to accept such a crown moulded out of the dirt and dregs of revolution, disloyalty and treason."
>
> Publicly he said that "If accepted, it demands from me incalculable sacrifices and burdens me with heavy duties. The German National Assembly has counted on me in all things, which were calculated to establish the unity, power and glory of Germany. I feel honoured by their confidence . . . but I should not justify that confidence if I, violating sacred rights, were without the voluntary assent of the crowned princes of our Fatherland, to take a decision which would be of decisive importance to them."'

Frederick William's rejection of its offer effectively ended the Frankfurt parliament. Although there was disorder in many parts of Germany in the early summer of 1849 in support of the parliament, it was quickly put down by the armies of the rulers.

There were a number of reasons why the Frankfurt parliament was unable to unite Germany:

1. There were serious differences about what sort of German state should be created. The workers who had helped to get the revolution going by rioting in Berlin, Silesia and the Rhineland (and who were represented by a minority at Frankfurt) did not want a monarchy controlled by middle class electors. They wanted a republic which would protect workers against their employers. The middle class nationalists were their employers, and they claimed that their businesses would not survive if they agreed to this.

Economic and social pressures may have helped to bring about the 1848 revolution, but the ambitions of the different social groups were contradictory.

2. It was almost impossible to agree what area would be incorporated in the united Germany. Would it include Austria (the 'Grossdeutsch' or Greater German solution) or would it exclude Austria on the grounds that her main interests were elsewhere (the 'Kleindeutsch' solution, aiming at a Little Germany)? The parliament only reached a conclusion in early 1849 after the Austrian Emperor regained control of his lands and made it clear that Austrian power depended on Germany remaining divided, and that he would not agree to any form of unification.

3. There had not been enough active unrest in 1848 to force the rulers of the German states to give up their thrones or control of their armies. They made concessions which could later be taken back, bided their time and, when the revolutionary tide receded elsewhere (especially in Austria), they used their armies to restore their authority. This made it clear that Germany could not be united by powerless members of an elected parliament, with neither a civil service nor an army which could be relied on to obey its orders. If Germany were to be united, it would have to be done by the power of one or more of the existing states. Golo Mann explains the failure of the 1848 revolution to unite Germany in this way:

> 'Unlike the French in 1789, the Germans in 1848 rebelled against well-run, powerful states. Their demand was for greater freedom for the individual, control of the government by popular representatives, and above all for national unity. A nation becomes one by feeling itself to be one. The Germans in the middle of the nineteenth century clearly had this feeling. The Frankfurt Assembly never put to the German princes the basic question of all struggles for power: can you kill me or can I kill you? The assembly's aim, its language, its way of life had been to reconcile the old with the new. The defeat of the revolution justified those who regarded such an attempt as nonsense and who believed only in force.'
>
> (*The History of Germany Since 1789*)

Prospects for German unification in the 1850s

When the revolutions were over, German nationalism seemed a spent force. The unusual combination of economic distress and the uprisings across Europe had aroused great popular enthusiasm in Germany for unification. But the events of 1848 and 1849 seemed to show that German nationalism was too weak and divided to achieve its aims by pressure from below, and enthusiasm quickly evaporated among the newer converts. However, there remained the possibility of unification from above. Around 1850 it seemed that Prussia was willing to do this, but lacked the necessary power.

King Frederick William IV of Prussia was still very interested in the idea of a united Germany, although he had shown in 1849 that he did not want a Germany in which the ruler was controlled by his people. As soon as the Prussian army had extinguished the last flames of revolution, Frederick William took up a scheme for a federation of states in which the army and foreign policy would be controlled by Prussia. This would basically be a 'Kleindeutschland', although Austria would be allowed to be part of a parallel organisation with few powers and little meaning. The first 'Parliament' of the new federation met at Erfurt in March 1850, but only a few small states joined Prussia. The others either distrusted Prussia's motives or were frightened by the likely reaction of Austria, which was now recovering fast from the revolutions under a strong new chancellor, Prince Schwarzenberg.

Austria objected strongly to a plan which would have ended her power in Germany, and persuaded a majority of the states to meet at Frankfurt in May 1850 to plan the restoration of the pre-1848 German confederation. Schwarzenberg said 'We shall not let ourselves be thrown out of Germany.' In the confrontation which followed, Prussia had to give way. Prussia feared that the Austrian army was too strong; in addition the Austrians had a promise from the Russian emperor that his army could also be used against Prussia. At a meeting with Schwarzenberg at Olmutz in November 1850, the Prussians agreed that their union should be abolished. Prussia was humiliated by having to give way so completely to threats of force by Austria. The meeting at Olmutz showed that Austria was politically much stronger than Prussia in 1850, and suggested that there was little prospect of real unification of Germany while Austria did not want it.

The military and political power lay with Austria, and an empire which included as many nationalities as the Austrian one did could not afford to encourage nationalism by permitting the unification of Germany.

Austria now attempted a knock-out blow against Prussia. Schwarzenberg's aim, he said, was to 'Let Prussia be humiliated and destroyed.' He planned to bring to an end the German customs union (the Zollverein), which was dominated by Prussia, and to replace it with a wider customs union including and controlled by Austria. The smaller states would not accept this plan, which accordingly collapsed in 1852. The customs union with Prussia gave them benefits which they were not willing to endanger, showing that, although Austria might still be stronger politically, it was Prussia which was stronger economically.

The 1850s saw a growth in the trade and industry of Germany in general and of Prussia in particular which made the customs union with Prussia more important than ever to the smaller states. These statistics show how Germany's industry was growing in the 1850s in comparison with Austria's:

	Coal production		Pig iron production	
	Annual average (in million tonnes)		Annual average (in thousand tonnes)	
	Germany	Austria	Germany	Austria
Late 1840s	6.1	0.8	184	146
Early 1850s	9.2	1.2	245	173
Late 1850s	14.7	2.2	422	266

Length of railways open (in kilometres)		
	Germany	Austria
1840	469	144
1845	2143	728
1850	5856	1579
1855	7826	2145
1860	11,084	4543

The growth of Prussia's own trade and industry in the 1850s was particularly impressive. For example, the number of joint stock companies founded in Prussia rose from thirty-seven by 1850 to 144 by 1859. Coal production in Prussia's Ruhr coalfields rose from 1,961,000 tonnes in 1850 to 8,526,000 tonnes in 1865. In 1846 there were thirty-three engineering works in Berlin, employing 2821 workers. By 1861 there were sixty-seven, employing 6313 workers. The weight of goods carried by Prussia's railways increased six times between 1850 and 1860. Because of the Zollverein, much of the railway-building boom of the 1850s involved railways which linked Prussia to the other German states.

As Prussia's economic power grew in the 1850s, the trade links of the other German states with her became more important than ever. On the other hand, Austria's political power declined in the 1850s. She had failed to support Russia in the Crimean War (1853–56) and so had lost an ally which in the late 1840s had helped her to put down revolutions in her own territories and to bring the other German states to heel. In 1859 the Austrian army performed poorly in a war with France and Sardinia in northern Italy. The relative power of Austria and Prussia seemed very different in 1860 from in 1850. It is not surprising that German unification began to look a more practical proposition again in the late 1850s, and that an increasing number of nationalists began to look to Prussia to bring it about.

In 1859 the middle class lawyers, officials, merchants and teachers who had always been the most faithful nationalists were encouraged to set up a new organisation. It was called the 'Nationalverein'. Its aims can be seen in a statement issued in August 1859:

> 'The present dangerous situations of Europe and of Germany have brought together from the various German states a number of men to come to an understanding about the establishment of a constitution for a united Germany and about the necessary course of action for the attainment of that aim.
>
> It is necessary that the German Federation should be replaced by a firm, strong, permanent central government and that a German national assembly should be summoned.
>
> In the present circumstances effective steps can be taken only by Prussia. It is the duty of every German to support the Prussian government. We expect all patriots in the German Fatherland to work together.'

ESSAY

Choose one of the following views on the growth of German nationalism after 1815, and write an essay to discuss it.

1. 'In the thirty years after 1815 there were some factors which were favourable to German nationalism and the unification of Germany, but far more which were unfavourable.'

2. 'Economic developments did more than writers and thinkers to encourage German nationalism between 1815 and the 1850s.'

3. 'The events of 1848–49 showed just how weak German nationalism was in the mid-nineteenth century.'

4. 'In the 1850s no one would have believed that Prussia and not Austria would unify Germany.'

Bismarck and German unification

On 18 September 1862 the Prussian ambassador to France, Otto von Bismarck, received a telegram from Berlin. It read 'Hurry. Delay is dangerous.' Three days after he had taken the train to Berlin, Bismarck was made minister-president of Prussia. King William I was unable to agree with the Landtag (the Prussian parliament) about how the army was to be reformed. Bismarck's commission was to find a way to solve the quarrel, which threatened to lose the king his throne.

Nine years later William was the emperor of a united Germany. Under Bismarck's leadership Prussia had fought three wars – with Denmark in 1864, with Austria in 1866, and with France in 1870–71. The result of these wars was that the various states of Germany were united in one empire under Prussian leadership.

These dramatic and rapid developments raise several issues:

1. What was Bismarck's aim when he became minister-president of Prussia in 1862?
2. Was it largely because of Bismarck's skill and daring as a statesman that Germany was united?
3. What part did nationalism play in the unification of Germany?
4. Did Bismarck have a master plan, which mapped out exactly how he was going to unify Germany, or was he a skilful opportunist who took full advantage of events as they unfolded?

These issues are all connected. They raise questions about the *authority* of Bismarck and the Prussian state on the one hand and of the other German states on the other hand; and about the *ideology* and sense of *identity* of different groups of people in Germany.

TASK

Look for evidence in this chapter to show:

1. how much Bismarck did to bring about the unification of Germany.
2. things which helped Bismarck to unite Germany, e.g. nationalism; the wealth of Prussia and the power of its army; the policies of the major powers of Europe; and the

mistakes made by Bismarck's opponents. (You will also find information on some of these in Issue 2.)

The four issues listed at the beginning of this chapter will give you lines of enquiry which will help you to think about the evidence.

Note and organise the evidence you find.

Bismarck and the struggle between King William and the Landtag

In the summer of 1862, when he was still the Prussian ambassador to France, Bismarck went to London to see the International Exhibition. He attended a dinner at the Russian Embassy. One of the Russian diplomats wrote in a book in 1887 an account of the conversation he said Bismarck had had at that dinner with Disraeli, leader of the Conservative Party, which was then in opposition in Britain:

> '"I shall soon," he said in effect, "be compelled to undertake the conduct of the Prussian Government. My first care will be to reorganise the army with or without the help of the Landtag... As soon as the army shall have been brought into such a condition as to inspire respect, I shall seize the first best pretext to declare war against Austria, subdue the minor states and give national unity to Germany under Prussian leadership."'

This is certainly what Bismarck did and, if we can believe this account, he was already planning it in 1862. Some historians have argued that, on the contrary, he had no real intention of unifying Germany when he became minister-president. A modern historian, Bruce Waller, suggests that:

> 'This is unlikely since it offers no other explanation for Bismarck's ascendancy than the notion that he followed a lucky star. Bismarck was indeed lucky, but this does not in itself explain his achievements. We must think of an explanation which will allow for a considerable amount of planning and foresight, but also for flexibility, irrationality and downright opportunism as well.'

It is certainly true that in 1862 Bismarck seemed to have more pressing problems than how Germany would eventually be unified. When he became minister-president, he had to work for his royal master to find a way out of a quarrel with the Prussian Landtag which had lasted for two years and was becoming more and more bitter. This quarrel was apparently over the improvement of the Prussian army. King William wanted to strengthen it in a number of ways – the most important being to increase from two to three years the period that all young men in Prussia had to spend in the army. What a majority of the Landtag bitterly opposed was the way in which the army was to be strengthened.

The Landtag objected to the reforms for a number of reasons.

Firstly, many of the members of the Landtag were liberals, who believed that everybody should have as much freedom as possible and that at least the wealthier and better educated people should have a say in choosing the government. They were afraid that if young men were in the army for three years, they would be drilled and disciplined to obey like robots all the orders that they were given. Most of the officers who would give the orders were junkers (Prussian landowners), who believed that Prussia should be run by the king and landowners as it always had been. The liberals in the Landtag were afraid that the army could be used against them if they demanded a greater say in how Prussia was run.

Secondly, many of the members of the Landtag were also nationalists, who wanted to see Germany united as soon as possible. They had been greatly excited by the unification of Italy in 1859–60: Austria had been defeated in northern Italy and then Garibaldi had landed in Sicily with a small and ill-equipped force ('The Thousand') and had marched north to bring the whole of southern Italy into a united country. If Italy could be united so quickly, why not Germany? However, many of the members of the Landtag did not see unification coming the same way as it had done in Italy. They thought that if the Prussian king and army were brought under the control of elected representatives of the wealthier citizens (the sort of parliamentary government which already existed in Britain), then the other states of Germany would voluntarily join with Prussia to form a united Germany. For example, the Prussian People's Union was set up in 1861 to campaign for seats in the Landtag and to:

'offer a hand to like-minded men in the wider German Fatherland. They have agreed with one mind and one voice upon the following main points:
1. Unity of our German Fatherland, yet not like the Kingdom of Italy by blood and fire, but by the union of our princes and peoples.'
. . .

They believed this was not going to happen if the army were reformed in such a way as to increase the power of the king and the junkers, whom they thought were more interested in preserving Prussia as it was.

By 1862 the Landtag was threatening to cut off taxes if King William would not compromise over the planned three-year army service. When he refused to do this, a deadlock seemed to have been reached.

The quarrel was not only about army reforms. There were very serious issues at stake – issues concerned with the *authority* of the Prussian state and the *ideology* and sense of *identity* of its citizens.

At one point, it seemed to King William that there was no way out but for him to abdicate the throne. The king saw that his call to Bismarck to come back to Berlin in September 1862 was possibly his last chance. He had not always agreed with Bismarck in the past, but he regarded him as a man of intelligence and determination who might be able to solve his problem.

Here is how Bismarck remembered in later life his interview with the king after he had arrived from Paris:

'The King asked me whether I was prepared as minister to advocate the reorganisation of the army, and when I agreed he asked me further whether I would do so against the wishes of a majority in the Landtag. When I said I was willing, he finally declared, "Then it is my duty, with your help, to attempt to continue the battle, and I shall not abdicate."'

Bismarck's first attempt to solve the King's problem was to try again to reach a compromise agreement with the Landtag. When this failed, he collected the taxes without the Landtag's approval. This was against the constitution (– the rules which had been laid down for governing Prussia) and so was quite illegal. 'I foresee how it is all going to end,' the king is said to have complained to him, 'they will cut off your head and a little later mine.' Bismarck is supposed to have replied, 'How better to die, I struggling for the cause of my king and Your Majesty for the right belonging to you by the grace of God.'

Bismarck's aims in 1862

It was obvious to all that Bismarck was following a very risky policy in collecting taxes illegally and in ignoring the objections of the Landtag to the army reforms. What we need to work out is what his aims were in following this policy and how carefully he calculated in 1862 and 1863 how he and the king could break free from their problems. It is usually thought that he gave a hint of his intentions as early as 29 September 1862 in a very famous speech which he made to the Landtag:

> 'The great independence of the individual makes it difficult in Prussia to rule with the constitution. We are perhaps too educated to put up with a constitution: we are too critical. However, Germany does not look to Prussia's liberalism, but to its power. Bavaria, Württemberg, Baden can indulge in liberalism, but no one will expect them to undertake Prussia's role. Prussia must gather and consolidate her strength in readiness for the favourable moment, which has already been missed several times. Prussia's boundaries according to the Treaty of Vienna (1815) are not favourable to a healthy political life; not by means of speeches and majority verdicts will the great decisions of the time be made – that was the great mistake of 1848 and 1849 – but by iron and blood.'

It has been suggested that the following aims can be seen in this speech:

The defence of the king

There is no doubt that Bismarck was determined to defend the powers of the king against the liberals. He said in another speech to the Landtag in January 1863:

> If you had the right to fix what the Government is allowed to spend; if you had the right to demand of His Majesty the King the dismissal of those ministers in whom you have no confidence; if you had the right to fix the size and organisation of the army . . . then you would indeed have full control of the government. We shall untiringly defend the rights of the Crown against your claims.'

In Figure 3.1 you will see a cartoon from a German liberal magazine. Bismarck is saying about the constitution, 'I cannot rule with this'. The cartoonist has put on Bismarck's head the spike from the top of a Prussian officer's helmet, suggesting that he might use the army to rule without the constitution.

The unification of Germany

Many historians now believe that Bismarck's calculation was that if he could bring about one of the Landtag's wishes (the unification of Germany), he would be allowed to ignore its other wish (control of the government). According to this view, what he meant by 'Prussia's role' in his 'iron and blood' speech was to unify Germany. Prussia would not unite Germany by peaceful persuasion, as the liberals envisaged, but by force or by the threat of force. This would meet the aspirations of all those who craved for a united Germany. It would offer glittering business prospects if the industries which were growing rapidly in the different states

Das Unzulängliche,
Hier wird's Ereigniß.

Fig 3.1 A cartoon showing Bismarck's attitude to the constitution.

could all be within a united Germany. If all this could be achieved, the liberals would not press their demands for parliamentary government.

War with Austria

Some historians have argued that if this was Bismarck's plan, he must have intended to use the 'iron and blood' against Austria. Prussia could only unite Germany under her leadership by destroying Austrian power in Germany. They argue that Bismarck knew from the outset that his gamble could come off only if he could exclude Austria from Germany by war or by the threat of war.

We will now consider whether Bismarck believed that war with Austria was inevitable, and whether he had a carefully worked out plan, as he is supposed to have claimed to Disraeli in 1862.

How flexible was Bismarck's policy?

Some historians have not accepted that Bismarck was planning from 1862 to unite Germany, or that he would necessarily come into conflict with Austria. One of these, William Carr, wrote:

'Had Austria recognised the ascendancy of Prussia in North Germany and her right to expand at the expense of the smaller states, Bismarck would willingly have recognised Austria's predominant position in Southern Germany. The new minister-president was not bent on war with Austria. His diplomacy was much more subtle, flexible and many-sided than his utterances sometimes suggest. War was obviously one solution to the rivalry with Austria – and probably the most likely outcome, but he firmly believed that war should be resorted to only as a last resort when all hope of a peaceful solution had been abandoned.'

(*A History of Germany 1815–1945*)

A number of historians have suggested, as in this extract, that Bismarck's policy was very flexible, that he always had two irons in the fire and that he waited to see how events would turn out before deciding his next move. He did not control events, but was influenced by them. On the other hand, it does not seem very likely that (as this writer suggests) his aim was merely to establish Prussia's control over north Germany. This would not have solved the problem which was the starting point of his policy. To divide Germany between Prussia and Austria would have made unification seem further away than ever – which would have horrified the German nationalists in Prussia and would have been likely to provoke the show-down with the Landtag that he was trying to prevent.

The exclusion of Austria from Germany

In 1863 began a sequence of events which can be seen, with hindsight, as leading to the exclusion of Austria from any power or influence in Germany. There is no doubt that this would be necessary if Germany were to be united under Prussian leadership. You will have to reach your own conclusions about how far Bismarck had a detailed plan for this, and how far he responded to events as they unfolded.

Prussia helps Russia against the Poles

In February 1863 Bismarck committed Prussia (under the Alvensleben agreement) to help to put down a revolt in the Russian part of Poland.

It has been suggested that his aim was to make sure that Russia did not support Austria against Prussia in the struggle which he saw coming. If he was trying to get Russian support, the move almost backfired, as Russia was at first offended by his inter-ference. In any case, the days were already long gone when Russia (as in 1848–49) would help Austria in her times of trouble. Austria's failure to support Russia in the Crimean War had ended their friendship.

If Bismarck as early as 1863 was trying to win support from the powers of Europe, his move was no great success. Britain and France were countries where the national feeling of the Poles was much admired, and both Britain and France were angered by Bismarck's determination to put down the Polish revolt. As a great power on Germany's western border, France's agreement would be vital if Austria were to be excluded from Germany.

Perhaps Bismarck's real concern in early 1863 was that since there were Poles in the Prussian province of Posen, the revolt might spread to them. He was certainly no friend of the Poles. In 1861 he wrote in a private letter:

> 'Strike the Poles so that they despair for their lives. I have every sympathy for their plight, but if we want to survive we cannot but exterminate them.'

The Congress of Princes

In August 1863 almost all of the German rulers met at Frankfurt, on the invitation of Austria, to discuss the reform of the German Confederation.

Figure 3.2 shows them arriving at a banquet. Each coach had in it the ruler of a separate German state. Notice that there are more coaches entering the square from the street beyond.

*Fig 3.2   German rulers
arriving at a banquet
during the Congress of
Princes.*

Even when speaking to the princes of the separate states,
Emperor Francis Joseph of Austria felt he had to pay some
attention to the nationalist movement for German unification. He
told them that:

> 'The time has come for renewing, in the spirit of the times, the
> German Confederation. We shall give new vigour to it and
> enable it to uphold to the end of time the honour, power,
> security and welfare of Germany as one great and inseparable
> whole.'

He did not suggest that the separate states should disappear.
What he proposed was that a 'directory' of five men would have
powers to act over the whole of Germany. As the architect of the
scheme, Austria would obviously play the leading part in ruling
Germany through the directory.

In the event, the plan was never carried out. Bismarck with
great difficulty persuaded King William not to attend the Congress
of Princes. William felt that it was wrong that the king of Prussia
should not take his proper place in this glittering gathering, but
Bismarck believed that any scheme agreed by the princes was
bound to be to Prussia's disadvantage. There was a tearful scene,
during which Bismarck (not for the last time) threatened the king
that he would resign. As a result, William did not go to Frankfurt.
And without Prussian participation, the plan had no chance of
being carried out.

This turned out to be one of the last opportunities for Austria to
reassert her leadership in Germany. For the German princes it was
the end of an era. They were never to meet again in this way.

War with Denmark over Schleswig–Holstein, 1864

Later in 1863 there was uproar among nationalists throughout Germany when the duchies of Schleswig and Holstein were made more fully part of Denmark. Most of the people of Holstein and half of the people of Schleswig spoke German; and, although they had long been under the Danish crown, they had previously enjoyed special privileges. German nationalists now demanded that they should become a separate state under the German Duke of Augustenburg. In December 1863 the smaller states made a start on this by using their armies to establish the duke in Holstein.

In January 1864 Prussia and Austria intervened and soon occupied Schleswig and Holstein. It was not until October 1864 that Denmark finally made peace and agreed that the duchies should be passed to Prussia and Austria. Prussia and Austria had at first opposed the Duke of Augustenburg, but in June 1864 they had said that the duchies would be liberated under him. However, Bismarck now insisted that the duke's army and navy must be controlled by Prussia. The Austrians believed that they had been tricked, and there was much talk of war between Austria and Prussia. But this did not come yet. In August 1865 their relations were patched up in the Convention of Gastein: Prussia would administer Schleswig and Austria would administer Holstein until a final settlement could be made.

It is not easy to work out what Bismarck was trying to do in the very complicated diplomatic and military moves over Schleswig–Holstein. It has been suggested that it was all part of his master plan to unify Germany under Prussian leadership. At Gastein, it is said, he manoeuvered Austria into a position in which he could pick a quarrel with her any time he liked over the administration of the duchies. Evidence about his motives is given in a letter he wrote in December 1863 to the Prussian ambassador to Russia:

'The question is whether we are a Great Power or a state of the German Confederation. The pursuit of the phantom of popularity in Germany has cost us our position in Germany and in Europe. If we were to throw ourselves into the arms of the small states, we should be led instead of leading. We can gain strength only from the politics of a Great Power equipped with suitable weapons, and we have not sufficient power to dissipate it on the wrong cause or on phrase-making or on the Duke of Augustenburg.

    For the moment I regard it as the right policy to have Austria on our side; whether the moment for separation arrives and on whose part we shall see. I am not afraid of war – on the contrary.'

Clearly this was an occasion when Bismarck made no effort to win the support of the German nationalists. It was Prussia's power he wanted to expand. In contrast, the nationalists wanted an independent Schleswig–Holstein under the Duke of Augustenburg, and were furious at the part he played. However, his diplomacy in this period is so complicated that it is difficult to believe he was doing more than waiting for events to unfold which he could use to his advantage. If he was determined to have war with Austria, he could have had it in 1865 and would have had no need to paper over the cracks in the Convention of Gastein.

The Austro–Prussian War, 1866

Those who see Bismarck as the master planner believe that war with Austria was delayed till 1866 to give Prussia time to get the international support which she would need. This they say was begun when Bismarck met and reached an understanding with the French emperor, Napoleon III, at Biarritz in October 1865. It was completed, they say, in April 1866 when Italy agreed to attack Austria from the south, in return for a promise that Austria would be forced to give up Venetia (Venice and the surrounding area) to her. But it seems more likely that what really happened was that events played into Bismarck's hands.

The international situation was in fact favourable to Prussia throughout the early 1860s. Britain was wary of interfering in continental affairs at this time. We have seen that after the Crimean War Russia was not likely to help Austria. Throughout this period Napoleon III dreamed of reshaping Europe into national states: France, therefore, was likely to be favourable towards Prussia. However, Napoleon III's policy tended to be erratic and, since no definite agreement seems to have been made at Biarritz, it was still tantalisingly uncertain in 1866 how far France would back Prussia. Italy at any point in the mid-1860s was likely to seize the opportunity to complete her unification by fighting Austria for Venetia.

Perhaps in 1865 and in early 1866 Bismarck was not yet sure whether he would have to go to war with Austria to establish Prussian domination of Germany. Perhaps he was keeping his options open, waiting for events to develop and hoping that Austria might give him what he wanted without war. This is what he himself claimed years later. In 1890 he said:

'A statesman is like a man wandering in a forest who knows his general direction but not the exact point at which he will emerge from the wood. It was difficult to avoid war with Austria, but he who is responsible for the lives of millions will shrink from war until all other means have been exhausted.'

Austria's mistakes

Austria had already made one mistake in acting with Prussia in Schleswig–Holstein. It is difficult to see what long-term gains she could have hoped to have made by interfering in an area on the north coast of Germany far from her own border. In 1865 and 1866 Bismarck was engaged in a game of brinkmanship and was willing Austria to make more mistakes. She duly did so in late April 1866. News of Italian troop movements panicked her into mobilising her southern armies. This enabled Bismarck to persuade King William to agree to mobilise the Prussian army. On 7 June Prussian troops entered Holstein. On 10 June Bismarck put forward plans for a new German state which would exclude Austria, and for a German national assembly to be called to create the new state.

Austria was provoked into going to war with Prussia. Saxony, Hanover, Bavaria, Hesse, Württemberg and Baden came into the war on Austria's side.

Bismarck was now eager publicly to court the support of German nationalists in a way that he had not done before. The Prussian proclamation on the outbreak of war said:

> 'The German Confederation for half a century has represented and promoted, not the unity, but the fragmentation of Germany. A majority of its members abolished the Confederation when they decided to arm against Prussia. All that remains is the living unity of the German nation. It is the duty of governments and peoples to find a new means of expressing this unity and one with the strength to last.
>
> Let the German people, with this high aim in mind, come forward in confidence to meet Prussia. Let it help to promote and make secure the peaceful development of our common Fatherland.'

Prussia, therefore, was fighting for a modern unified Germany. Whether she was able to bring it about depended on the power and efficiency of her army.

The Prussian and Austrian armies

Up till now the Prussian army had been regarded by many in Europe as a rather comic parade ground army. But it marched west and south and soon overran Hanover, Hesse and Saxony. The real test came when the Prussians entered Bohemia and faced the Austrian army at Koniggratz. The armies were well matched. The Austrians had more artillery pieces and they had a longer range. The Prussians suffered badly from this in the early stages of the battle. A Prussian soldier whose unit was stationed among the houses of a village remembered that:

> The shells crushed through the clay walls as if through

Fig 3.3   The Battle of Koniggratz in 1866.

cardboard, and finally raking fire set the village on fire. We withdrew to the left into the woods but it was no better there. Jagged hunks of wood and big tree splinters flew around our heads. We all felt we were in God's hands.'

On the other hand, the Prussians were better organised. The commander was Helmuth von Moltke, who had been in charge of the reform of the Prussian army since 1860. He made sure that orders were quickly and efficiently passed to the units which were to carry them out. The Prussian infantry also had better methods of fighting and better weapons. They advanced in small groups, firing their needle-guns and then lying down to reload. These needle-guns were more accurate and faster firing than the Austrian infantry weapons. The Austrians rushed forward packed together and had to reload in a standing position. They were, therefore, much easier to hit than the Prussians were.

Figure 3.3 shows the battle and illustrates the account you have just read of how the Austrians and the Prussians fought. The battle is being fought at the foot of the valley. The soldiers on the hill in the foreground are fresh Prussian soldiers joining the battle. The Prussians are advancing in small groups on the left-hand side. The Austrians are packed together on the right-hand side.

What finally decided the battle was when, according to plan, another Prussian army arrived and started to surround the

Austrians. When Moltke saw this, he said to King William, 'The campaign is decided. Vienna lies at Your Majesty's feet.' The Austrians managed to pull 180,000 troops out of the trap, but these soon degenerated into a rabble. *The Times* correspondent saw the Austrians that evening:

> 'Wounded on all sides, fragments of regiments marching, the roadsides lined with weary soldiers asleep, dressing their wounds or cooling their feet, on both sides of us wagons, guns, cavalry of all kinds . . . the debris of an army.'

Koniggratz involved more men than had ever before fought in a European battle. Its consequences were to be equally momentous.

Prussia's victory was due to the efficient organisation of her army and to her growing economic power, which we examined in Issue 2.

Bismarck, although he was a civilian, was also on the battlefield. He said before the battle 'If we are beaten, I shall not return. I can die only once, and it befits the vanquished to die.' This was rather theatrical, but it was true that his position and the chance that Prussia would unify Germany depended on this day's fighting. Ironically, no accommodation had been arranged for him, and he spent much of the night of his triumph outdoors in extreme discomfort. That he did not sleep was also because he was now worrying about the other major uncertainty in the great gamble he was taking – the attitude of France.

France's attitude

Napoleon III had expected a long war between Prussia and Austria, which would have weakened both. He was shocked to hear the news from Koniggratz, and immediately wrote to King William proposing an armistice. The king and his generals were in no mood to listen. They had the bit between their teeth and were ready to march on Vienna. They had dreams of a victory parade through the Austrian capital. Bismarck was appalled and wrote to his wife:

> 'If we are not excessive in our demands and do not believe that we have conquered the world, we will attain a peace that is worth our effort. I have the thankless task of pouring water into the bubbling wine and making it clear that we do not live alone in Europe but with three other powers that both hate and envy us.'

Napoleon followed up his request for an armistice with concrete proposals (to which Austria had agreed). The old German Confederation would be ended. A new North German Confederation would be set up which would be dominated by Prussia. Bismarck now had another of the tearful scenes with King William, in which he threatened the king with his resignation. This is what he remembered saying to the king in the *Reflections and Reminiscences* that he wrote in the 1890s:

> 'We had to avoid wounding Austria too severely; we had to avoid leaving behind her any unnecessary bitterness of feeling or desire for revenge; we ought rather to reserve the possibility of becoming friends again with our adversary of the moment. If Austria were severely injured, she would become the ally of France.
>
> The King said that the chief culprit should not be allowed to escape unpunished. I replied that we were not there to sit in judgement, but to pursue the German policy. Our task was the establishment of German national unity under the leadership of the King of Prussia.'

Historians who regard Bismarck as the master planner of German unification have seen this as evidence that he deliberately gave Austria easy terms because he saw that this would help his next move. The reason, they say, was that he knew Prussia would eventually have to fight a war with France before she could unify the whole of Germany under her leadership. He knew that Prussia could not win this war unless Austria remained neutral.

However, something that Bismarck wrote at the time to King William is easier to believe:

> 'By Your Majesty's acceptance of the proposals of His Majesty the Emperor of the French, the danger of France's taking sides against Prussia has been eliminated.
>
> Austria's declaration that it will withdraw from the German Confederation and recognise everything Your Majesty thinks fit to do in North Germany provides all the essentials that Prussia demands of her.
>
> In my humble opinion it would be a political blunder to put the whole outcome in jeopardy by attempting to wrest from Austria a few more millions of war payments, and expose it to the risk of a prolonged war or negotiations from which foreign interference could not be excluded.'

This suggests that Bismarck did not persuade King William to accept the peace terms because he had a clear plan for his next move. It implies that he needed a quick peace to avoid losing everything. The French army might soon be mobilising on the Rhine. The Austrian troops which had been victorious on the Italian front might soon be brought north of the Alps. This was the time to take what was on offer before the situation turned against Prussia.

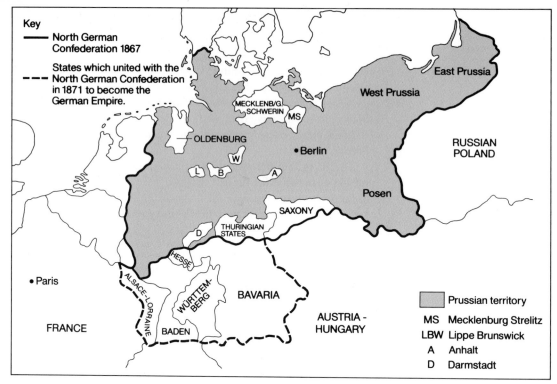

Key

—— North German Confederation 1867

- - - States which united with the North German Confederation in 1871 to become the German Empire.

MECKLENB/G.SCHWERIN

MS

OLDENBURG

W

•Berlin

East Prussia

West Prussia

RUSSIAN POLAND

L   B   A

Posen

SAXONY

•Paris

D   THURINGIAN STATES

HESSE

ALSACE-LORRAINE

WÜRTTEM-BERG

BAVARIA

AUSTRIA - HUNGARY

FRANCE   BADEN

▨ Prussian territory

MS Mecklenburg Strelitz
LBW Lippe Brunswick
A   Anhalt
D   Darmstadt

Fig 3.4   The making of the German Empire.

The North German Confederation

In the peace settlement made in August 1866 Austria agreed to two new German confederations being set up. As you can see from Figure 3.4, the North German Confederation made up the greater part of Germany. Most of it was by now Prussian territory. In 1866 Prussia had annexed Schleswig-Holstein and a number of other states (the most important being Hanover). A few smaller states in the North German Confederation (such as Saxony) remained theoretically independent, but were now dominated by Prussia. For example, Prussia controlled the confederation's army.

The southern states were to be framed into a much looser South German Confederation.

The old German Confederation (which had included German Austria) was abolished. This and the decisive way in which Austria had been defeated by the Prussian army meant that Austria no longer had any influence at all in the way Germany was governed.

Bismarck's policies all seemed to be coming to fruition. Prussia had excluded Austria and now dominated a large part of Germany. As he had hoped, this won him the support of most of the liberals and nationalists in the Prussian Landtag. Many had still been very critical of him up to 1866, but after that he was on much better terms with most of them. A month after the war had ended, the Landtag agreed to pass a bill which excused the government for collecting taxes illegally since 1862.

Bismarck had been correct in gambling that most of the liberals would do without parliamentary government in return for the definite prospect of German unification.

Bringing in the southern states

To complete the unification of Germany, all that remained was to combine the southern states – Bavaria, Baden, Württemberg and Hesse – with the North German Confederation. Bismarck claimed in later life that from 1866 he had a definite plan to bring this about by means of a war with France. In his *Reflections and Reminiscences* he wrote that:

'I assumed that a united Germany was only a question of time, that the North German Confederation was only the first step in its solution. I did not doubt that a Franco-Prussian War must take place before the construction of a united Germany could be realised. I was at that time preoccupied with the idea of delaying the outbreak of war until our military strength should be increased.'

Some historians believe that Bismarck did indeed plan a war with France from 1866. As we have seen, they say that this is why he was not too harsh in making peace with Austria. This, they say, is also why he made a secret treaty with the south German states in 1866, in which they agreed that their railways and armies would pass under Prussian control if an attack was made on Germany. As France was the only country likely to attack Germany, this can be seen as preparation for war with her. Otto Pflanze is one of the historians who has taken this view:

'Bismarck's goal was . . . a crisis with France. He deliberately set sail on a collision course with the intent of provoking either a war or a French internal collapse. The partisans of his innocence ask us to believe a most improbable case: that the shrewdest diplomatic mind of recent history permitted Germany to be drawn into a war which he was eager to avoid.'

Other historians believe that Bismarck would have been happy to unify Germany without war with France if that could have been managed, and that between 1866 and 1870 he was keeping his options open and waiting for events to develop in a way which he could exploit. Bismarck wrote in a letter to the Prussian ambassador to Bavaria on 26 February 1869:

> 'That German unity could be promoted by actions involving force I think is self-evident. But there is quite a different question and that has to do with bringing about a powerful catastrophe and the responsibility of choosing the time for it. There is a danger of shaking down unripe fruit, and that German unity is not ripe fruit at this time leaps to the eye.'

Which of these views historians take determines how they explain the way in which Bismarck used the choice of a new king of Spain to bring about the final moves towards the unification of Germany.

The Hohenzollern candidature

In September 1869 the vacant Spanish throne was offered to Leopold of Hohenzollern, a member of the Catholic branch of the Prussian royal family. Leopold was unenthusiastic, and at that stage no Prussian pressure was put on him to accept. The outcome was different when the offer was renewed in February 1870. When the offer became public knowledge in July 1870, Bismarck claimed that the Prussian government 'had had no knowledge of these proceedings'. However, this letter from Bismarck to King William (written in March 1870) was found in the secret files of the German foreign office after 1945:

> 'Your Majesty will I trust permit me to summarise in writing the motives which in my modest opinion speak in favour of an acceptance of the Spanish Crown by the Prince of Hohenzollern.
>
> I am of the opinion it would serve Prussian and German state interests if he accepts. For Germany it is desirable to have on the other side of France a country on whose sympathies we can rely and with whose feelings France is obliged to reckon. We have in the long run to look for the preservation of peace not to the goodwill of France but to the impression created by our position of strength.'

There is now plenty of evidence to prove that Bismarck did his utmost to persuade the unwilling Leopold to accept the Spanish throne. What he was up to is shown by the diary of one of his agents, who met Leopold and his father on 19 June. He wrote that, although the prince agreed, 'there came various scruples. What would France say about it? Would it not give rise to complications? I said, "Bismarck says that is just what he is looking for."'

In 1870 Bismarck was clearly using the question of the Spanish throne to stir up trouble with France. Some historians believe that he was deliberately provoking France into a war which would lead to the unification of Germany. Others say that he was encouraging a crisis with France in the hope that he could turn it to his advantage by peaceful means, and that war was only a last resort. W. N. Medlicott has commented that:

> 'Some historians have recently tried to prove either that the whole affair was an example of brinkmanship which went wrong, or even that Bismarck's aims were peaceful and defensive, and that no one was more surprised than he at the result... What we seem to have in this case is an example of Bismarck's skilful pursuit of alternative courses. There were two possibilities; either that France would agree to the Hohenzollern election, in which case Prussia would be no worse off... or France would not, in which case there might be a war, for which he was ready. What we must reject is that he was innocently unaware of this second possibility.'

Whatever his motives earlier, there is no doubt that when the secret of the Hohenzollern candidature leaked out in July 1870, Bismarck wanted war. The French government played into his hands by objecting to the candidature in very strong terms. The French foreign minister Gramont said in a speech:

> 'We do not believe that respect for the rights of a neighbouring people obliges us to allow a foreign power to put one of its Princes on the throne of Spain to alter the present balance of power in Europe to our disadvantage and to endanger the interest and honour of France. This we firmly hope will not happen. If things fall out otherwise, strong in your support and that of the nation, we shall know how to do our duty without hesitation and without weakness.'

Nationalist feeling was outraged throughout the whole of Germany, including the southern states. All the German prejudices against the French (going back to the invasion by Napoloeon l's armies in the early 1800s) came bubbling to the surface. This was the perfect background for a war of national unification. However, the opportunity was almost lost in an incident which shows that Bismarck was not always the master of events (even in Prussia). The French ambassador Benedetti met King William at his summer holiday resort, Ems. William (who had never been keen to force his relative to accept the Spanish throne) told him that the family was reconsidering the matter, and soon Leopold announced that he was standing down. Prussia seemed to have been humiliated, and Bismarck claimed later that he had considered resigning. However, at this stage his plans were rescued by the folly of the French government, which now demanded of King William that he would promise never to allow the Hohenzollern candidature to be renewed. William refused in polite terms, but his telegram from Ems reporting on what he said was edited by Bismarck to sound like a humiliating snub:

'The French ambassador in Ems demanded that His Majesty pledge himself for all future time never again to give his consent to the prince resuming the candidature. His Majesty has thereupon declined to receive the ambassador again and has informed him through an adjutant that he has nothing further to communicate to the ambassador.'

Bismarck produced this edited version while he was dining with the two leading Prussian generals, Moltke and Roon. He claimed later that he told them (to their great delight) that, 'it will have the effect of a red rag upon the Gallic bull. Fight we must unless we wish to play the part of the vanquished.' This was certainly the result. France declared war on the North German Confederation on 19 July.

The Franco-Prussian War

The German armies mobilised very speedily, from the south as well as from the north. A wave of patriotism swept through Germany. A writer expressed the general feeling in this way: 'Any German, whoever he may be, who is not now on the side of his people is a traitor.'

This proclamation issued by King William on 25 July is full of references to German patriotism:

'From all the tribes of the German Fatherland, from all the circles of the German people . . . I have received so many messages of devotion and willingness to make sacrifices on the occasion of the coming struggle for the honour and independence of Germany . . . that I express my royal thanks and add my assurance that I shall return the loyalty of the German people with my own eternal loyalty. The love for our common Fatherland and the unanimous uprising of the German people and their princes have reconciled all differences and opposition; and, unified, as seldom in her history, Germany will find that the war will bring her lasting peace and that, out of the bloody seed, will come a God-blessed harvest of German freedom and unity.'

The armies of the southern states cheerfully marched to fulfill the secret treaty of 1866 (see page 59), by which they were bound to fight with north Germany. In Figure 3.5 Bavarian dragoons are seen cheering as they pass the headquarters of the Crown Prince of Prussia. As in 1866, Bismarck was greatly assisted by the power of German nationalism.

Within eighteen days 462,000 German troops had been gathered on the French frontier. This was made possible by the very effective use of the railway system which had been built up in Germany. Figure 3.6 shows Prussian dragoons about to leave

Fig 3.5 Bavarian dragoons cheering as they pass the headquarters of the Crown Prince of Prussia.

Fig 3.6 Prussian dragoons leaving Berlin by train for the front in 1870.

Fig 3.7 A Prussian ammunition train.

Berlin for the front, and Figure 3.7 shows a Prussian train taking munitions to the front in 1870.

The French mustered their army more slowly along congested and disorganised railways, and on the eighteenth day of the war had in the field only half the number of troops that the Germans had. This allowed the German armies to invade France while their enemy was still unprepared. The Prussians soon got between Paris and the two main French armies. By 3 September one of these French armies had been trapped at Metz and the other (with Emperor Napoleon III) had been forced to surrender at Sedan. The emperor was immediately deposed and a new French Republic was proclaimed.

The war dragged on until Paris was bombarded into surrender at the end of January 1871. By this date the policy of Bismarck and the ambitions of the German nationalists had already been fulfilled. It was obvious to the southern states that they could not afford to stay out of such a powerful state as Germany had now become. Bismarck reached terms with the rulers of these states for them to join with the North Confederation to form a united Germany. On 18 January 1871 (when the shells were still raining down on Paris), William was proclaimed German Emperor in the Hall of Mirrors at Versailles. A German account written shortly after reflects the spirit of the occasion:

'By the self-sacrificing devotion of all classes of society, the nation has proved that it still possesses that warlike prowess which distinguished our ancestors. It has recovered its ancient position in Europe and accepts the destiny prophesied for it in the proclamation of its new Emperor. This destiny is to add to its power, not by conquest, but by promoting culture, liberty and civilisation.

The King walked up to where the colours were displayed and, standing before them, read the document proclaiming the re-establishment of the German Empire. Count Bismarck having read the King's proclamation to the German nation, the Grand Duke of Baden [one of the southern states] stepped forth and exclaimed "Long Live His Majesty the Emperor." The cheers of the assembly were taken up by the bands playing the national anthem.'

This was certainly a triumph of German nationalism, but it was also seen by Germans as a triumph for Bismarck. A picture of the scene in the Hall of Mirrors, which was published soon after in *The Illustrated London News*, showed the principal figures standing in a row being cheered by the soldiers. However, Figure 3.8 is the one which Germans hung up in their homes. It shows the new Emperor on top of the steps on the left-hand side. The figure in the centre of the picture is a tall man in a white uniform and long military boots. He stands with his feet apart surveying proudly the result of his labours. It is Bismarck.

Fig 3.8   The proclamation of William I as the German Emperor at Versailles.

ESSAY

Choose one of the following views about Bismarck's part in the unification of Germany and write an essay to discuss it.

1. 'Bismarck was a master statesman who worked out in 1861 how he would unify Germany, and carried out his plan.'

2. 'It is a mistake to over-emphasise the contribution of any one man to an important historical process. Germany would have been united without Bismarck.'

3. 'There was nothing inevitable about the unification of Germany. Although Bismarck made the most of his chances, he would not have succeeded without good luck.'

The German state, 1871–1914

The German Empire which was proclaimed with such pomp and pride at Versailles in 1871 lasted less than fifty years. It collapsed in November 1918 when the First World War ended in the defeat of Germany and the flight of Emperor William II to Holland. The short life of the German Empire has led historians to wonder whether there were fatal flaws in it from the outset. Was there something radically wrong about the way in which Bismarck established it and tried to control it as chancellor until 1890? Or were his successors at fault for failing to understand and manage effectively the system which he had set up? We can divide these questions into several issues:

1. Was power in the German Empire too concentrated in Prussia and its landowners in general, and in the emperor and the chancellor in particular?
2. Would the empire have been stronger in the long run if it had been less authoritarian and if Bismarck had allowed a wider range of people to feel that they were involved in decision-making?
3. Alternatively, should Bismarck be congratulated for preserving the empire in its vulnerable early days by playing off against each other the many political groups and forces in Germany?
4. Did Bismarck's successors after 1890 fail to keep up his political balancing act?
5. In particular, did Emperor William II cause confusion by failing to give a consistent lead?
6. In the late nineteenth century industry and large towns grew more rapidly in Germany than ever before. Did this bring such rapid social change that Bismarck's way of ruling Germany could not have been expected to continue unaltered?
7. Did the German Empire allow itself to be drawn to its doom in the First World War because it seemed to be a way of evading the demands of the growing class of industrial workers for more rights?

These issues raise questions about *authority* in the German Empire, and about the *ideology* and sense of *identity* of different groups of people in Germany.

TASK

Work in groups.

Imagine that it is November 1918. Germany has been defeated in the First World War. Some German soldiers are discussing what went wrong. They are all men who, for one reason or another, are well informed about events in Germany since 1871. Each tries to explain from his own point of view how Germany was governed between 1871 and 1914, and whether he thinks this form of government was good for the country.

One or two members in each group can take the part of one of these soldiers:

Number One is the son of a Prussian landowner. He was an army officer before the First World War began.

Number Two is the son of the owner of a coalmine in the Rhineland. He was a university student before the war began.

Number Three worked in an engineering works in Berlin. He was a local organiser for his trade union and for the Social Democratic Party. His father died of typhus soon after the family moved to Berlin from the Pomeranian countryside to look for work.

Number Four was a Catholic school teacher in Bavaria.

Make notes on what your character would think about the way in which Germany had been governed between 1871 and 1914.

Explain your point of view to the other members of the group. And make notes on the points of view of the other members of the group.

Bismarck and the German state, 1871–90
Bismarck and the constitution

Rules on the way in which the German Empire was to be governed were laid down in the constitution of 1871 (which was almost identical to the constitution drawn up for the North German Confederation in 1867).

All forward-looking states in the nineteenth century were expected to have a constitution. It showed how the powers of the ruler and his servants had been limited and usually provided for some form of elected assembly to scrutinise the actions of the ministers who made up the government. Constitutions were particularly favoured by liberals. As we have seen in previous chapters, they believed that everyone should have as much freedom as possible and that at least the wealthier and better educated people should have a say in choosing the government. For liberals, a constitution was vital as it laid down who should have a say in the government and how.

At various times Bismarck claimed to be a believer in constitutions. It was certainly he who framed the constitution of the

German Empire, and in some respects it went even further than
the liberals wanted it to do in giving people the vote.

There were two assemblies. The Reichstag was elected by all
men over the age of twenty-five. A recent writer on Bismarck,
Bruce Waller, has explained Bismarck's motives in this way:

> 'Bismarck believed that a constitution with a liberal colouring
> would appear to be modern and so help to ensure support from
> the educated public. If it were, in addition, "anointed with a
> drop of democratic oil" [the vote for all men over the age of
> twenty-five] it would appear progressive as well and tie the
> common man to him. Bismarck was convinced that the healthy
> peasant or man in the city street had traditional views and could
> be used as a counterweight against the aspirations of the liberal
> middle class.'

(*Bismarck*)

Every year the Reichstag had to approve the budget, which laid
down what the government would raise in taxes and how it
would spend them.

The Bundesrat was made up of men appointed by the twenty-
five states within the empire, such as Prussia, Bavaria, Saxony,
Baden, Württemberg, and so on. The Bundesrat was supposed to
show that Prussia had not simply taken over the other parts of
Germany. New laws were to be approved by the Reichstag and
the Bundesrat, as well as by the emperor and the chancellor (the
head of government).

Some people argue that this constitution was a mere sham, a
fig-leaf designed to hide Bismarck's determination that Germany
would be ruled by the Prussians in general, and by the emperor
and his chancellor in particular. These people see the government
of the German Empire (like that of Prussia before it) as very
authoritarian, expecting complete obedience. A German wrote at
the time that:

> 'It is a common error among newcomers to Berlin to take for
> real the assemblies here. One quickly realises that Germany has
> a fine façade of a constitutional system, with turmoils in the
> corridors, lively debates and defeats inflicted on the
> government. However, behind the scenes, at the back of the
> stage, intervening always at the decisive hour and having their
> way appear the Emperor and Chancellor.'

It is certainly true that the popularly-elected Reichstag was not
in a strong position. Its most important power was to pass or
reject the budget. Even so, Bismarck was able strictly to limit its
say in the most important area of spending – on the army. The
Reichstag could not dismiss the chancellor or any of his ministers,
who were appointed by the emperor and were answerable only to
him and to the Bundesrat.

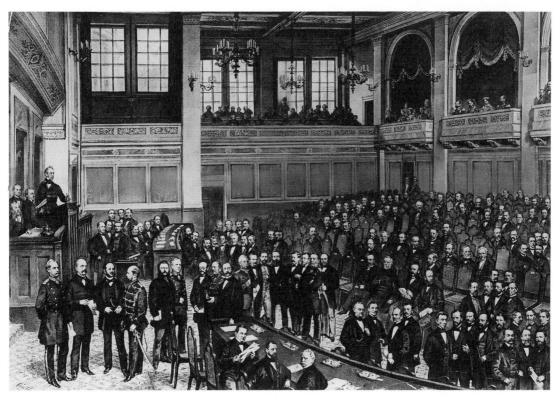

*Fig 4.1   The German
Reichstag in 1871.*

Figure 4.1 shows the Reichstag in the early 1870s. You will see
that it was not at all like the British House of Commons, where
the government and the opposition sit facing one another. This
was because the government was quite separate from the
Reichstag.

With the exception of the budget, the Reichstag's decisions
could be overturned by the Bundesrat. However, the voting
system in the Bundesrat was such that in important matters it was
controlled by Prussia. The king of Prussia was always the emperor
of Germany, and the emperor was in almost complete control of
foreign policy and the army.

It is therefore easy to suggest that the constitution was designed
to give the impression that power was shared with the people as a
whole and with the different German states, but that the truth was
that Prussia (represented by the emperor and the chancellor)
exercised the real control. Bismarck often complained of the self-
will of the emperor, and there were indeed noisy scenes between
them. But as long as William I was on the throne, his worst fear
was that Bismarck should resign (as he regularly threatened to
do), and so Bismarck always got his own way in matters on
which he was sufficiently determined.

Other people argue that Bismarck's Germany was not as authoritarian as it might seem. They believe that Bismarck's main
concern after 1871 was to preserve the empire he had created.

What he was doing, they say, was to balance the different political forces in Germany until all Germans felt themselves to be really part of the new state. One liberal politician summed up this view in a speech in 1881:

> 'We must strive for as much freedom as the national state can tolerate. By and large, Prince Bismarck represents for me the determination to keep a national state. I do not always like his methods. But in the face of all this I remind myself that nobody else has such a lively regard for the idea of making the young empire vital, permanent and resilient. All his twists and turns and inconsistencies can be explained by the power of this idea.'

Historians who accept this point of view have argued that there were many signs in Bismarck's Germany of a modern state which allowed its people to express their views and which paid attention to the people. There was a free press. The law was fair and generally respected. Political parties flourished and put great efforts into publicising their views and attracting votes. Those who were elected to the Reichstag were not without influence. Bismarck would not have put so much effort over the years into trying to keep a majority in the Reichstag if it had counted for nothing.

We will now consider how Bismarck governed Germany by examining his relations with the most important political groups.

Bismarck and the National Liberals

The National Liberals were those liberals who thought that the unification of Germany was as important as their liberal beliefs. When the defeat of Austria in 1866 offered the prospect that Prussia could unite Germany, it was they who had agreed to a law excusing the Prussian government for having collected taxes illegally since 1862. They were the largest party in the first Reichstag of the empire (elected in 1871) and it was natural that they should co-operate with Bismarck's government in the 1870s in measures which made Germany more genuinely united. The same currency and weights and measures were to be used throughout the empire. Businesses throughout Germany were to obey the same rules. Law courts were to operate in the same way, and a start was made to bring together the laws of the different states. The railways were extended to link all parts of the empire.

The National Liberals had no difficulty in agreeing with the government on these matters. Not only would these measures unite Germany; they would also encourage free competition in trade. The National Liberals were mostly well-educated and wealthy men, like bankers, merchants and civil servants, who fervently supported free trade. Bismarck also needed the backing of the National Liberals in the 1870s in his struggle with the

Catholic church (see page 72). They supported him because liberals wanted to reduce the power of churches.

What is clear is that Bismarck in the early 1870s was certainly not the mouthpiece of the Prussian landowners (the junkers). Many of the junkers disliked policies which they thought would increase the importance of the merchants and factory-owners, and destroy the independence of Prussia and the power of religion.

However, Bismarck certainly did not feel bound to follow the views of the National Liberals merely because they were the largest party in the Reichstag. He seems to have felt uncomfortable that this impression might be given, because the National Liberals agreed with him on so many matters. In 1879, after their co-operation had collapsed, he felt able to say this in a speech to the Reichstag:

> 'Since I have been a Minister I have never belonged to any party and have not been able to belong to any party . . . from the beginning of my career I have had only one guiding star: that is, by what means and in what direction I could bring about German unity and . . . how I can consolidate this unity, how I can promote it and shape it in such a manner that it will be maintained permanently . . . I am not an enemy of the constitutional system, on the contrary I regard it as the only possible form of government, but if I believed that a dictatorship in Prussia would have been more useful for promoting German unity, I would have advised that.
>
> If after 1871 I was forced into closer dependence on the Liberal Party than is perhaps in the long run desirable for a minister and chancellor, I could not for that reason give up for ever all relations with other groups in the Empire . . . I cannot, and the government cannot, be at the beck and call of particular parties. It must go its own way that it regards as correct; these courses are subject to the resolutions of the Reichstag, the government will require the support of the parties but it can never submit itself to the domination of any single party.'

If taken at face value, this speech would seem to support the view that Bismarck's policy was not authoritarian, but was designed to strengthen German unity by balancing the different forces in the empire. It suggests that he recognised the need to have the support of the Reichstag. On the other hand, he struggled hard with the Liberals in 1874 to keep out of the Reichstag's control the most important item of government spending – money for the army. The army budget (which had last been granted in 1867) had to be renewed by the Reichstag in that year, and Bismarck demanded that it should be granted on a permanent basis. This would mean that the Reichstag would never again be able to vote on the taxes to pay for the army. This particularly offended the Liberals, who believed that the Reichstag should have as much control as possible over the government. In the end Bismarck agreed to a compromise that the military budget should be granted for seven years at a time. This did not give the Reichstag very effective control over army spending. It suggests that Bismarck was not very sincere in saying that 'the government will require the support of the parties', and it also suggests that the Liberals did not feel that they were in a strong bargaining position, even though they were the largest party in the Reichstag.

Bismarck and the Catholics

Although Prussia and the North German Confederation had some Catholic subjects in the Rhineland and in the Polish parts of the eastern provinces (such as in Posen and West Prussia), their peoples were mainly Protestant. However, the entry of the southern states into the German Empire in 1871 meant that about a third of the inhabitants of the empire were now Catholics.

It might seem obvious that a leader determined to hold together the new empire should set out to prove that Catholics would not be second-class citizens. To be fair to Bismarck, the circumstances of the time did not make this easy. Pope Pius IX was afraid that in the rapidly changing Europe of the late nineteenth century the Catholic Church was losing its traditional power. He fought back at the modern world by declaring in 1870 that any statement that he made about the faith had to be accepted by Catholics everywhere. He might give instructions to the German bishops, which they would be obliged to obey. This concerned Bismarck, who was determined that his government should be obeyed by everyone in the new empire.

In the first elections for the Reichstag of the empire in 1871, fifty-seven seats were won by the Centre Party, which had been set up to protect German Catholic interests. The Centre Party had the second largest number of seats (after the National Liberals). Bismarck was very alarmed, not only because the first loyalty of the Centre Party might be to the Pope, but also because the Centre Party supported the cause of the overwhelmingly Catholic Poles of the eastern provinces, where Polish nationalism was growing fast. It is not surprising that Bismarck saw the Centre Party as a possible danger to the empire that he had created.

When he had decided to act, Bismarck did so with characteristic energy. In 1872 he banned from Germany the most active order of Catholic priests, the Jesuits, and introduced a new law that only the government would have the right to inspect schools (including Catholic schools). Further laws against the Catholic Church followed in 1873. The government would control the training of priests and appoint them to churches. No one could be married without a civil ceremony in a government office. Bismarck claimed that he was not trying to prevent Catholics from following their religion. Here is how he argued this in a speech he made in 1873:

> 'It is not a religious but a political question. It is not, as our Catholic citizens are being told, a struggle of a Protestant ruler against the Catholic Church. It is not a struggle between belief and unbelief... [If the Pope had had his way] we would have had, instead of the German Empire which was being developed, two political organisations running Germany – one with its general staff in the Centre Party, the other with its general staff in the government and person of His Majesty the Emperor. This situation was a totally unacceptable one for the government, and it was its duty to defend the state against this danger.'

However, the Catholics did not see it this way. They saw it as an attack on the religious beliefs of a substantial minority of the citizens of the empire. This feeling that Bismarck was trying to destroy the Catholic Church in Germany is reflected in Figure 4.2.

Fig 4.2   Cartoon of Bismarck and The Devil.

In this cartoon the Devil asks Bismarck how long he thinks it will take him to pull down the church. When he says three or four years, the Devil replies, 'I've been at the same job for the last eighteen hundred years; but, if you can do it in three or four, I will resign my office in your favour.'

Zwischen Berlin und Rom.

Der letzte Zug war mir allerdings unangenehm; aber die Partie ist deshalb noch nicht verloren. Ich habe noch einen sehr schönen Zug in petto!

Das wird auch der letzte sein, und dann sind Sie in wenigen Zügen matt — — wenigstens für Deutschland.

Fig 4.3   Cartoon of Bismarck and Pope Pius IX playing chess.

The 'Kulturkampf'

To Bismarck's surprise the Catholics did not accept his church laws, but fought back. The result was the 'Kulturkampf' (or 'struggle over civilisation') between Bismarck on the one hand, and the Centre Party, the Catholic Church and Pope Pius IX on the other. Bismarck found Pope Pius to be a clever and determined opponent. Figure 4.3 is a cartoon which shows them as well-matched chess players.

It became clear quite soon that Bismarck was not winning the struggle. In the 1874 Reichstag elections the Centre Party increased its strength to ninety-one seats. However, Bismarck was determined to impose his will, and the contest continued year after year.

Bismarck's motive in starting the Kulturkampf was certainly to protect the empire he had created. But his determination to win the contest actually weakened the empire in these ways:

Firstly, it weakened the loyalty of Catholic citizens.

Secondly it offended Prussian Conservatives (mostly the junkers on whom the army depended for its officers). These tended to be staunch Protestants, and so would not have been expected to be friends of the Catholics. However, they objected to a German government which tried to control what had previously been decided at local level. They also objected to laws which had the effect of reducing the powers of all the churches.

And finally, it had implications for the future of German Jews. Bismarck's main support in the Kulturkampf came from the National Liberals, who believed that religion should play no part in the running of the country. Many of the leading National Liberals were Jews, and the unpopularity of the Kulturkampf rubbed off on them. There were also other reasons why Jews were becoming increasingly unpopular among some Germans. For example, there was envy at their success in building businesses as the economy grew.

Bismarck changes course in the late 1870s

By the late 1870s it was at last clear to Bismarck that he must make peace with the Centre Party. He could no longer deny even to himself that the Kulturkampf was causing damage. The way he did it gives support to the view that Bismarck's basic instinct was to protect the empire by balancing the various forces of which it was made up. When he was really in difficulty, it is argued, this is what guided the way he ruled Germany.

But was he in difficulty in the late 1870s? Here are some of his problems:

Firstly, the Centre Party had survived his attack and had actually slightly increased its seats in the Reichstag (to ninety-three) in the 1878 elections.

Secondly, the Conservatives (representing the Prussian land-owners who supplied the officers for the army and some of the factory-owners who supplied its guns) were increasingly unhappy with Bismarck's policy. As we have seen, they disliked the Kulturkampf for their own reasons. They were also suffering more and more from the very low customs duties charged on goods coming into Germany. This free trade policy was very much approved by the university teachers, bankers and merchants who led the National Liberals. Indeed it was central to their beliefs. However, since 1873 prices had been falling throughout the world. For Prussian landowners it meant that their incomes dropped as steamships brought in more and more cheap grain from the wide plains of the USA – Bismarck was himself one of the landowners who suffered in this way. For German factory-owners, it meant that they were struggling for survival against British firms which were still larger and more up-to-date than they were. In 1878 the Conservatives increased their seats in the

Reichstag from seventy-eight to 115 and they criticised Bismarck more and more fiercely for keeping to the National Liberal policy of free trade.

In addition, the imperial government was very short of money. It could have tried to raise extra funds from the state governments (Prussia, Bavaria, Baden, and so on). However, Bismarck was keen to find ways of raising the taxes which came directly to his government.

Finally, Bismarck was becoming increasingly unhappy that he had to rely on one party in the Reichstag (the National Liberals), especially since that party believed that the government should eventually be controlled by the Reichstag.

After the number of National Liberal seats had dropped from 127 to ninety-eight in the 1878 Reichstag elections, Bismarck saw his way clear to solving several of his problems and to maintaining the balance in the empire at the same time. He gradually changed direction by abandoning the National Liberals and by relying instead on the Centre Party and the Conservatives. To win the votes of the Centre Party he had to begin to reverse the laws against the Catholic Church. Many historians have been astonished by the complete lack of shame with which he carried out this about-turn. For example, Gordon Craig comments that:

> 'Erick Eyck, in his biography of Bismarck, has described the way in which the Chancellor, during this process, made speech after speech in which he blandly contradicted everything he had said earlier in defence of the laws that were now being repealed. It is doubtful whether any other European statesman of his age could have carried this off without suffering so much in reputation that he would be forced to resign. But Bismarck never lacked self-assurance, and he was too pleased by the success of the political manoeuvre to be concerned over the other effects of his religious policy. One is tempted to compare him with that Earl of Cardigan who led the Light Brigade into the Russian guns at Balaclava and then retired in good order himself, leaving ruin and destruction behind him.'
>
> (*Germany 1866–1945*)

It has been suggested that Bismarck taught Germans to admire dishonest statesmanship, with serious consequences in the twentieth century when Hitler came on the scene. This is a question we will return to later (see page 99).

If Bismarck was to do without the National Liberals, he also had to win the votes of the Conservatives. To do this he had to abandon free trade and introduce much higher customs duties on goods entering Germany. This would also solve the financial problems of the imperial government. In the long run this decision was probably even more important for the future of Germany. It was followed by a rapid growth in German industry which had important effects on many aspects of German life. This is how he justified the decision to protect German farmers and factory-owners in a speech to the Reichstag in 1879:

> 'The only country [which persists in a policy of free trade] is England, and that will not last long . . . Therefore to be alone the dupe of an honourable conviction cannot be expected of Germany for ever. By opening wide the doors of our state to the imports of foreign countries we have become the dumping-ground for the production of these countries . . . Since we have been swamped by the surplus production of foreign nations, our prices have been depressed; and the development of our industry and our entire economic position has suffered in consequence.
>
> Let us finally close our doors and erect some barriers . . . in order to reserve for German industries at least the home market, which, because of German good nature, has been exploited by foreigners.'

Bismarck and the industrial workers

We have seen in Issue 2 that until 1850 there were few large factories in Germany and that most Germans were still country-dwellers. However, industry grew rapidly in the 1850s and 1860s, and by 1870 a third of all Germans lived in the towns and cities. In the early 1870s factories were being set up and peasants were moving into town to work in them faster than ever. Figure 4.4 shows the Krupp steelworks at Essen. You will see how large some German factories had become by this time.

Fig 4.4   Bird's-eye view of the Krupp steelworks in Essen in 1879–80.

There was a sudden halt to this growth in 1873 when throughout the world prices dropped and orders became harder to find. Many factories made workers redundant or even closed down. However, these workers could not go home to the countryside. Times were bad there also. They had to try to survive in crowded and dirty cities on lower wages or on nothing at all.

Poor conditions in the 1870s in the industrial towns led to increasing demands from the workers that they should be protected. In 1875 two existing workers' parties increased their demands and united to form a new party – the Social Democratic Party. They claimed to be Marxists, and said that their eventual aim was to end the empire and to set up a republic, which would take over the ownership of all the main industries in order to give the workers a fair share of the profits. However, for the moment at least, they were content to seek support in the ballot box, and in the 1877 Reichstag elections they won only 500,000 votes and just twelve seats.

Bismarck had a genuine fear of anything which threatened the existing owners of land or businesses. He was conscious that the Social Democrats won five times as much support in 1877 as the two previous workers' parties had got in the 1871 elections. He was convinced that if they continued to grow there would be a violent revolution. His first response to the Social Democrats was not to try to win them over, but (as earlier with the Centre Party) to try to crush them. His chance came in 1878 when two attempts were made to assassinate Emperor William I. Bismarck blamed the Social Democrats, and he had a law passed which curbed their activities. It seemed to him an added advantage of this law that it would divide the National Liberals at the very time when he was trying to weaken them. You will see from this extract from the Anti-Socialist Law why some of the liberals would object to it. Although they tended to support the employers, the liberals were also supposed to believe that everyone should be able to express their opinions freely.

'Organisations which through Social Democratic . . . activities aim to overthrow the established state or social order are hereby forbidden.

All meetings in which Social Democratic . . . activities appear to be dedicated to the overthrow of the existing state or social order shall be dissolved.

All publications in which Social Democratic influence appears to be aimed at overthrowing the established state or social order by breaching the public peace are forbidden.

Anyone who takes part as a member of a forbidden organisation shall be punished with a fine of up to 500 marks or with imprisonment of three months.'

This was not likely to make industrial workers feel that in Bismarck's empire they could make their grievances known and try to get them righted! It can be seen as another example of Bismarck's authoritarianism actually weakening the empire. As with his dealings with the Centre Party, his attempt to crush the Social Democrats was actually followed by an increase in their numbers and strength. About 1500 of them were imprisoned and many emigrated to America. However, the Social Democratic vote increased to over three quarters of a million in 1887.

Bismarck realised eventually that he had to do something to show that the empire could meet the needs of the industrial workers, as he had done with the Catholics. In the case of the workers, it was a very original system of state insurance against sickness and accident, with pensions for the disabled and for old people over seventy years of age. This was introduced between 1883 and 1889 – about twenty years before anything similar was done in Britain. Bismarck described this as a system of 'state socialism', and he justified the programme when he first introduced it to the Reichstag in 1881 as follows:

> 'We have been talking about the social question for 50 years. Ever since the passage of the anti-Socialist Law in 1878 I have been repeatedly reminded, both by persons in high official positions and by common people, that a promise had been given at that time that something positive would also be done to remove the causes of socialism.
>
> I think the state can be held responsible for what it omits to do. I do not think that a monarchy which is ruled for the good of the subjects can stand by and do nothing. Those who object to the state intervening in this way to protect the weak can be accused of wanting to use their wealth to take advantage of others.'

Bismarck believed that the industrial workers would be grateful to the state for the safety net which it now provided, and that Germany would, therefore, get a contented and well-behaved workforce. To some extent it did. There was no violent revolution until after the empire had been defeated in the Great War. However, Bismarck had expected state socialism to give him immediate and substantial benefits. He was very disappointed that he failed to win the hearts and minds of the workers, and that they voted for the Social Democrats in larger and larger numbers. Because of his alarm he proposed in 1889 that the Anti-Socialist Law should be made permanent. By now, however, Bismarck was finding it very difficult to control the Reichstag, which refused to pass the law. He also had to deal with a new emperor, William II, who believed that he could win over the workers by giving them a few more state insurance benefits.

DROPPING THE PILOT.

Fig 4.5   The cartoon 'Dropping the pilot', showing the dismissal of Bismarck by Emperor William II.

Bismarck's dismissal

Bismarck could no longer control the Reichstag or the emperor. His political balancing act, which had lasted for almost thirty years, was at last collapsing. After desperately trying to hold on to office, Bismarck was eventually dismissed by William II in March 1890. This extract from the letter that he wrote to the emperor shows that he was very hurt:

'I would have asked to be relieved of my offices to Your Majesty long ago if I had not had the impression that Your Majesty wished to make use of the experiences and abilities of a faithful servant of your ancestors. Since I am now certain that Your Majesty does not require them I may retire from political life without having to fear that my decision may be condemned as untimely by public opinion.'

There was a feeling abroad that William II was taking a great risk. Figure 4.5 is a famous cartoon showing William as a ship's captain dropping off the pilot. It appeared in the London magazine *Punch* only a few days later.

However, most people in Germany welcomed the new government. One historian, William Carr, has explained their feelings in this way:

'When Bismarck departed from Lehrter railway station on 29 March 1890, a squadron of hussars and a military band lined the platform. Ministers, ambassadors, generals and a crowd of admiring citizens cheered the old man and sang "The Watch on the Rhine" as the train steamed out of the station. But few Germans regretted his passing. There was much more concern in the foreign press than in Germany, where it was generally accepted that he had outlived his political usefulness. After "a first-class funeral", as Bismarck called it, Germany turned to the future with confidence under the dynamic young emperor and his chancellor, General Caprivi.'

(*A History of Germany 1815–1945*)

The German state under William II, 1890–1914

The character of William II

The new emperor was a man of many moods, and these moods were often contradictory. He could be charming in conversation and give people the impression that he understood their problems and would do his best to help them. It was probably because of this impression that most people in Germany welcomed the new government. On the other hand, William had a very firm belief in his right to rule and in his ability to make the correct decisions. In this letter that he wrote in 1892, he explained why he thought that he should ignore opposition:

> 'We Hohenzollerns are used to advancing slowly and painfully amidst troubles, conflict, party division and lack of appreciation. How often have my ancestors had to battle for policies in direct opposition to the will of the ignorant people, which first opposed and in the end blessed them. What do I care for popularity! I am guided only by my duty and the responsibility of my clear conscience towards God.'

William II gave the impression of being full of energy, and he was always rushing around giving his opinion on something or visiting somewhere. He was nicknamed 'the travelling emperor'. On the other hand, as a boy and as a man he never enjoyed serious reading, or studying books, or working through state papers. He boasted that he had never read the German constitution, and he certainly did not understand the background to many of the policies which had been followed by Bismarck. The result was that his views on important matters tended to be formed very quickly and without sufficient thought. They were often changed from year to year or even from month to month.

One very serious example of his lack of consistency was obvious from the beginning of his reign. As we have seen, he believed in 1890 that he could win over the industrial workers where Bismarck had failed, by using his charm and by giving them a few more state security benefits. But he was never particularly at ease in dealing with civilians of any class. Perhaps because he had been born with a wasted arm, his great ambition as a boy was to do well in physical exercises like riding and other military pursuits. He regarded himself as a soldier and spent much of his time among soldiers. This increased his tendency to expect automatic obedience. He was soon accusing industrial workers of being 'the enemy within the empire', because they voted for parties he regarded as his enemies. This was not the way to win their trust.

Bismarck's constitution gave the emperor (at least in theory) enormous powers. This had caused only occasional problems as long as Bismarck was working with William I. It was likely that the emperor (whoever he was) would wish to exercise more of these powers when the awe-inspiring figure of Bismarck had left the scene. It was unfortunate that, when the time came, the emperor was such an unstable character as William II. What added to the problems of running the empire smoothly was that at this time more Germans than ever before were moving from the countryside to the towns and cities to find work in factories. We have already thought about the effects of this in the 1870s and 1880s (see page 77), and we will now see how the problem became more acute after 1890. It has been suggested that Bismarck should have had the foresight to see these problems coming and that he could be criticised for governing the empire in a way which was unlikely to work after he had gone.

The growth of industry

The lower prices of the 1870s had slowed down the growth of German industry, but from the 1880s industry was again expanding rapidly. These tables show how Germany was performing in two of the most important industries in comparison with Britain (which had been far ahead of other industrial countries for over a century).

	Coal production (in million tonnes)		**Pig iron production** (in million tonnes)	
	Germany	UK	Germany	UK
1880	59.1	146.9	2.7	7.7
1890	89.3	181.6	4.6	7.9
1900	149.8	225.2	8.5	8.9
1909	217.4	263.8	12.6	9.5

The pig iron figures show that Germany was actually over-taking Britain in production of the material from which many finished products were manufactured.

Germany was particularly successful in developing sophisticated new finished products. For example, the electrical dynamo was invented by a German (Werner Siemens), and by 1913 Germany controlled almost half the world trade in electrical products. The development of the motor car in the 1890s was led by two Germans – Gottlieb Daimler and Carl Benz. And Germany was also very successful in developing its chemical industry. Whereas finished products made up only 38 per cent of German exports in

1873, they had risen to 63 per cent by 1913. The value of German exports rose threefold over the same period. The result was that by 1913 Germany's share of world trade was almost as great as Britain's. France, in comparison, had only half the share of either Germany or Britain.

Germany's success was based on ample raw materials in Alsace-Lorraine and in the Ruhr. It was also helped by forward-looking factory-owners and bankers, well-educated inventors and skilled workers. It was closely linked to the rapid growth in Germany's population from 41 million in 1871 to 65 million in 1911. In a country where the army was so important, the government did not want to lose potential recruits by letting too many emigrate and it did everything it could to encourage German industry. For example, in the early 1890s treaties were signed with Italy, Austria, Russia, Belgium and other countries, which reduced the customs duties on agricultural products (such as wheat) coming from them into Germany. German landowners suffered from this (at least in the short term), but in return these countries promised to accept German industrial products.

To find work, Germany's growing population had to move into the large towns and cities where the industries were now placed. In 1871 over 60 per cent of Germany's people were still country-dwellers, but by 1910 this figure had fallen to 40 per cent, and by then more people worked in industry than in agriculture. Industrial cities grew very fast – for example, Berlin grew from three quarters of a million people in 1870 to over two million in 1910. The factories demanded long hours of work and the cities could not provide good houses fast enough. After working for perhaps twelve hours, men often went home to conditions like those you can see in Figure 4.6. This photograph was taken in Berlin in 1910.

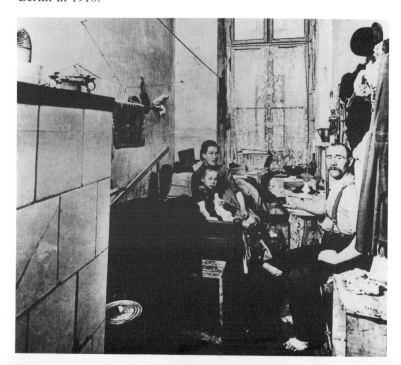

Fig 4.6   Living conditions for a worker in Berlin in 1910.

It has often been argued that these rapid economic and social changes meant that Bismarck's way of ruling Germany could not have lasted even if he had continued in office, for there were now simply too many tensions in the system for it to have continued unchanged.

The growth of the Social Democratic Party

As we have seen on page 78, the Social Democratic Party had been expanding since the late 1870s because it promised to improve the lot of the industrial worker. Its growth had not been halted by Bismarck's persecution or by his offer to the workers of 'state socialism'.

One of the reasons for Bismarck's fall had been William II's belief that he and not Bismarck could win over the workers. The result was the 'new course' followed by the new chancellor, Caprivi. Working hours were limited for many groups of workers (including all women, and boys under sixteen years old). Bismarck's laws against the Social Democratic Party were allowed to lapse. But William II was as disappointed by the results of his government's policy towards the workers as Bismarck had been in his time. When the Social Democratic Party was allowed to recruit openly, it grew faster than ever. It held a very well-attended series of congresses, which greatly alarmed the government by the language used by those attending. Figure 4.7 shows the congress at Halle in 1890. The slogan above the platform reads 'Workers of all lands unite.'

Fig 4.7 Social Democratic Party congress in Halle in 1890.

The Social Democratic Party adopted the following programme at Erfurt in 1891:

'The Social Democratic Party of Germany fights for the abolition of class rule and of classes themselves and for equal rights and duties for all (whatever their birth or sex). The Party makes these demands:

The vote for all men and women over 21;

The making of new laws and the appointment of high officials to be controlled by the people;

Decisions for war and peace to be made by the representatives of the people;

Religion is a private matter. The state should neither try to control churches nor give them money;

Justice to be free and judges elected by the people;

All taxes on goods to be abolished as they are an unfair burden on the poor;

The costs of the Government to be paid from income tax, property tax and inheritance tax, which would ensure that the rich paid most;

Eight hours to be the maximum working day and night work allowed only when there were pressing reasons for it.'

Not only the government, but also most of the factory-owners were alarmed by this programme. If it had been carried out, there would indeed have been a revolution. The landowners, officials and industrialists who shared power and influence with the emperor would have lost them entirely.

However, below the surface of the Social Democratic Party, things were not exactly as they seemed. The Erfurt Programme was accepted as a long-term aim in order to keep the party together. While many of its members really did believe in it, an increasingly important group was more interested in improving the lot of workers within the existing system. These were practical men rather than dreamers. They tended to be closer to the actual workers and were often officials of the trade unions, which were growing fast in the 1890s. They did not believe that there was any immediate prospect of the existing rulers and owners losing their positions. They wanted to help workers now by collecting funds to support the unemployed and by bargaining with employers for better wages and healthier working and living conditions. They wanted to win votes to build up their strength in the Reichstag and to persuade the government to give it more power. They believed that workers also were proud to be German and supported efforts to ensure that Germany was respected by other nations. These 'Revisionists' were an important group by the early 1900s. However, they never quite won the day, and on the eve of the Great War in 1914 officially the Social Democratic Party still believed in revolution.

The defenders of the existing order

It is clear that the landowners and factory-owners who claimed that any advance for the Social Democrats was a direct step towards revolution were wrong. They ignored what was going on inside the Social Democratic Party.

In the 1890s one of the leaders of the group which resisted any concessions to the Social Democrats was Baron von Stumm-Halberg, the owner of a large iron-making firm in the Saar. This speech that he made to his workers shows that he was unlikely to reach a compromise with the more moderate Social Democrats:

'I believe that we shall all continue to demonstrate that in the "Stumm kingdom", as our enemies sarcastically call our community, only one will prevails and that is the will of His Majesty the King of Prussia . . . It is frequently maintained that there is no comparison between industrial concerns and the army. I maintain the contrary. In both cases, if they are to be successful, discipline is essential. If an industrial enterprise is to flourish it must be organised in a military fashion. Just as soldiers from the Field Marshall down to the youngest recruit all take the field against the enemy united when their king calls them, so do the members of the Neunkirch factory stand together as one man when it is a matter of combating our competitors as well as the dark forces of revolution. If we win it is to the benefit of all of us; if we are defeated we all suffer from it and you certainly far more than I.

Any reduction in the authority of employers appears to me to be the more dangerous since a . . . reduction of authority in other fields, in state and church, will follow very soon . . . then it will not be long before authority is undermined where it is most necessary – in the army.'

There were some landowners and industrialists who genuinely did think that if any of their power were given up or if concessions were made to the Social Democrats, it would be a short step to revolution. There were many others who did not really believe this, but pretended to. They knew that the more moderate members of the Social Democratic Party would be happy to do a deal with them. However, as part of this deal they would have had to give up some of their power and to pay for better working and living conditions for their employees. They were not willing to pay the price. As a result, the moderates were never able to show the practical benefits of their approach – which might have made them the majority in the Social Democratic Party.

This is the view of those historians who believe that the German state between 1890 and 1914 suffered from a deep split between the workers who demanded greater rights and the land-owners and factory-owners who were unwilling to give up any of their power and wealth. In many countries the government would have forced each side to compromise for the general good. The German government followed no consistent policy.

Changes of direction in the emperor's policy

It is often claimed that Bismarck kept a rough and ready balance between the various political and social groups in Germany, with none being left too happy and none being left too unhappy. The emperor probably felt that he was maintaining this balance by allowing Caprivi to follow the 'new course' towards the workers in the early 1890s.

However, the emperor was both disillusioned and unnerved when in the Reichstag elections of 1893 the Social Democrats won forty-four seats and more votes than any other party. (They did not win most seats because the cities and large towns, where they tended to live, did not have a fair share of the seats.) He now changed course abruptly in a way which was to become characteristic of him. His speeches now included hysterical calls such as 'Forward into battle for religion, for morality and for order against the parties of revolution.' In 1894 Caprivi resigned in despair. His successor, Prince Hohenlohe, was himself of moderate views. However, he was not energetic enough to prevent the emperor's more extreme advisers from introducing laws to the Reichstag which would have made it a crime for anyone to stir up hatred between classes, or for workers to force fellow-workers to join a union or to come out on strike. But the Reichstag rejected both laws and insisted that they should be dropped. This was itself an interesting development, which would not have happened in Bismarck's time. However, it could not really be claimed that William II was achieving a balance. On the contrary, he was getting the worst of both worlds: he did not get his laws against the Social Democrats and the trade unions accepted, and he alienated the workers even more by saying that they were disloyal.

There was another change of course after 1899. The new chancellor, Bülow, was mainly occupied with foreign policy, and his secretary of state for the interior, Count Posadowski, was allowed to resume the policy of trying to satisfy the workers by making their lives easier. For example, accident and sickness insurance were improved. Work which could be done by children was limited again. In several cases these measures were agreed with the party leaders in the Reichstag before being introduced, and the Reichstag and the government then forced the Bundesrat to accept them. Many Germans expected that this trend would continue, and that the empire would gradually become answerable to the elected representatives of the people in the same way as the British government was answerable to the London parliament. Dependence on the Reichstag did continue between 1907 and 1909, when Bülow became the first chancellor to rule with the backing of a fixed group of parties. When in 1912 the Social Democrats won the votes of one in three Germans and became the largest party in the Reichstag (with 110 seats), there was some hope that a historic compromise between the rulers and workers of Germany might at last be in view.

Despite all William II's vacillations and the offence his views had given to his working class subjects, the situation was not explosive enough to suggest that a revolution was near. The Social Democrats might unite with some middle class Liberals to create a majority in the Reichstag and gradually push forward both the interests of the workers and the powers of the Reichstag over the government. William Carr has explained it in this way:

> 'It is true that a majority of the Reichstag favoured the revision of its powers to make it as powerful as its British and French counterparts. At the same time most members, including the Socialists, had the greatest respect for the monarchy and on that account made no attempt to force the pace of what seemed an inevitable movement towards parliamentary government. In short, there was much political tension and frustration in Imperial Germany – as in other countries in 1914 – but revolution was less likely here than elsewhere.'
>
> (*A History of Germany 1815–1945*)

In the event, moves to meet the workers' grievances and to lead Germany towards parliamentary government did not happen. The Social Democrats would not give up their revolutionary slogans. The Liberals did not feel that their middle class supporters would pay to improve the conditions of the workers. Most important of all, the emperor did not have a coherent policy to meet the grievances of his working class subjects. On the contrary, an incident in 1913 showed clearly that he and his advisers still believed that they could rule in the old authoritarian way.

The army was on bad terms with the French-speaking inhabitants of Alsace (annexed in 1871). When there was a demonstration against the local garrison in the town of Zabern, the commanding officer arrested twenty-eight citizens, including a judge and a lawyer, and locked them up for the night in the barracks. This was quite illegal and caused outrage throughout Germany. The emperor backed the army completely, refusing to accept any compromise and insisting that the only issue was whether the army had followed its own code of law. This gave the impression that in imperial Germany, the emperor and his army were superior to any civilian law. It is true that the army in particular and

uniforms in general were given exaggerated respect. The emperor himself was always seen in public in one of his many uniforms. Figure 4.8 shows him wearing one of them.

However, this did not really mean that in 1913 the emperor and his army were superior to civilian law. Nevertheless, it raises the question of whether the emperor and those around him were trying to put the clock back.

Some historians have argued that they were trying to distract the Reichstag and the workers from pursuing their demands by adopting an aggressive foreign policy. Whether they were trying to solve the social tensions of Germany by winning glory abroad and whether they deliberately brought about a war in 1914 to avoid social and political change in Germany are some of the questions we will discuss in the next chapter.

Fig 4.8   Emperor William II in one of his many elaborate uniforms.

ESSAY

Choose one of the following views about the way Germany was ruled between 1871 and 1914 and write an essay to discuss it.

1. 'Bismarck preserved the empire he had created by playing off against each other the different political groups in a masterly balancing act.'
2. 'The German Empire was flawed from the outset because power was too concentrated and Bismarck did not allow enough people to feel they were involved in decision-making.'
3. 'The real problem of Germany under William II was not the Emperor's inconsistency, but rapid social change, which was making the constitution of the Empire unworkable.'

Nationalism and German foreign policy, 1871–1914

Bismarck, Europe and the world, 1871–90

The leaders who drew Germany into two world wars in the twentieth century claimed that they were following Bismarck's nationalism and his belief in power politics. They said that his view, like theirs, was that the leading powers were bound to struggle for supremacy and that in doing so they could not be expected to pay too much attention to morality or fair play. We have seen that in uniting Germany Bismarck's policy was certainly aggressive, and that he exploited to the full opportunities offered by the weaknesses of his opponents. But is this a fair reflection of his foreign policy after 1871? In setting out to answer this question a number of issues need to be considered:

1. Are Bismarck's defenders right in claiming that his foreign policy after 1871 was nationalist only in the sense of having as its main aim the protection of the nation that he had created? Are they correct in saying that he managed to do this peacefully by diplomatic juggling as long as he was chancellor?
2. Alternatively, was he not constantly trying to get the better of the other Great Powers through a network of treaties and secret agreements, and was it not already clear by the late 1880s that this policy had failed because no one trusted him any longer?
3. Did Bismarck encourage Germans to accept and even admire a dishonest foreign policy?
4. When Bismarck eventually in the mid-1880s set out to win colonies, did this show a nationalistic desire to increase German power or was it simply a response to economic pressures and favourable opportunities?

These issues raise questions about the sense of *identity* of Germans in the 1870s and 1880s, and about the *authority* of Bismarck in Germany and of Germany in Europe and the world.

TASK

Work in groups.

Some groups will note down the evidence that Bismarck's foreign policy after 1871 was aggressive, or designed to raise tension, or dishonest.

Other groups will note down the evidence that his foreign policy was intended to defend the German Empire and the balance of forces in Europe.

Each group will make a presentation to the class of the evidence it has collected.

Discuss and make notes on the evidence found by the other groups.

The aims of Bismarck's foreign policy after 1871

Since Bismarck had launched three wars in six years, it was natural that observers in the early 1870s should assume that he would do so again. For example, the British ambassador in Berlin wrote in 1873:

'The two great objects of Bismarck's policy are:
1. The supremacy of Germany in Europe and of the German race in the world.
2. The reduction of the influence and power of the Latin race in France and elsewhere.

To obtain these objects he will go any lengths while he lives, so that we must be prepared for surprises in the future...
Germany is in reality a great camp ready to break up for any war at a week's notice with a million of men.'

The ambassador certainly put his finger here on one central feature of Bismarck's policy – the fear of France. Not only had France been defeated in a humiliating way by the German states in 1871, but she had also lost the provinces of Alsace and Lorraine to Germany, and she could be expected to take any opportunity to win them back.

Bismarck soon seemed to show that another of the ambassador's claims was correct – that he aimed to weaken France further.

By 1875 France was recovering surprisingly fast and high German officials (obviously prompted by Bismarck) hinted that Germany would launch a war against her to halt the recovery. A leading Berlin newspaper publicised the hints under the headline 'Is war in sight?'. The evidence is that Bismarck had no intention of declaring war and was simply trying to frighten France into slowing down the rebuilding of her army. However, Britain and Russia warned him against attacking France, and he had to climb down rapidly. This incident underlined forcibly a point of which Bismarck was already aware – that the German Empire must not allow itself to be isolated. He claimed that there was no reason why the other powers of Europe should combine against Germany. She was, he often repeated, a 'satiated nation', which did not want to win extra territory.

Some historians have in fact taken the view that Bismarck's policy after 1871 was not at all expansionist. For example, William Carr wrote that:

> 'As Bismarck monopolised the conduct of Germany's foreign affairs for nearly twenty years, German policy inevitably bore the imprint of his rather narrow view of international relations as a mere exercise in power politics. In an age of nationalism the German "national hero" closed his ears to appeals from Baltic Germans suffering under harsh Russian laws, and firmly resisted propaganda for the creation of Greater Germany; the multi-national empires of Russia and Austria were fixed points in Bismarck's diplomatic compass, anachronisms which it was in Germany's interest to preserve.'
>
> (*A History of Germany 1815–1945*)

On the other hand, he *was* nationalist in the sense of being determined to protect the new and vulnerable German Empire, and he believed that Germany must stress her peaceful intentions to prevent a coalition of Great Powers against her. This view is reflected in this extract from the *Reflections and Reminiscences* which he wrote in his retirement:

> 'There is the disadvantage of the central and exposed position of the German Empire, with its extended frontier which has to be defended on all sides and the ease with which anti-German coalitions are made. At the same time Germany is perhaps the single Great Power in Europe which is not tempted by any objects obtainable only by a successful war. It is in our interests to maintain peace. That respect for the rights of other states in which France especially has always been lacking at the time of her supremacy . . . is made easy for the German Empire in that we do not require an increase in our immediate territory. It has always been my ideal aim, after we had established our unity, to win the confidence not only of the smaller European states but also of the Great Powers, and to convince them that German policy would be just and peaceful, now that we had repaired the divisions of the nation.'

Bismarck's worry about coalitions of the Great Powers against Germany was natural enough since he had given them good reason to be afraid of him. He could live with France as a permanent enemy as he did not fear war against France alone. As it was generally assumed at this time that Britain would not fight a European war, the real danger for him was that France might ally with Russia or Austria–Hungary. The central points of his

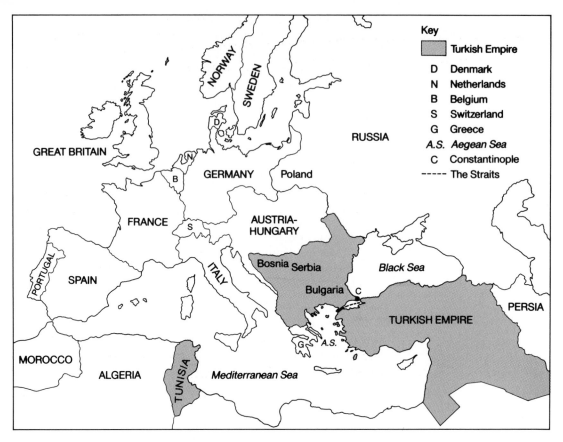

Key
▨ Turkish Empire
D Denmark
N Netherlands
B Belgium
S Switzerland
G Greece
A.S. Aegean Sea
C Constantinople
----- The Straits

Fig 5.1 Europe in 1871.

policy after 1871 were, therefore, to keep friendly with both Russia and Austria–Hungary and to ensure French isolation.

However, this was easier said than done. Russia still resented Austria's failure to support her in the Crimean War. There was now also a bitter rivalry between them to win territory from the decaying Turkish Empire in the Balkans (see Figure 5.1). Russia had a long-standing ambition to expand south towards Constantinople and the warm waters of the Straits and Aegean Sea (where her ships would be able to come and go without interruption by ice as at her northern ports and without interference by other countries). Austria, having been pushed out of Italy and Germany, was now very keen to make up her losses in the Balkans. There was, therefore, a constant risk of war between Russia and Austria–Hungary, which Bismarck was convinced Russia would win. However, he could not afford to let this happen. He believed that the collapse of the Austrian Empire would weaken other monarchies and might be followed by the unwelcome incorporation in Germany of large numbers of Catholic Austrians. If Austria were seriously threatened, Germany would have to fight to protect her. This would cause an alliance between Russia and France which could destroy the German

Empire. Therefore, to defend everything he had created, Bismarck believed that he must prevent Russia and Austria–Hungary from going to war. His foreign policy was, therefore, nationalistic in the sense that his main aim was to protect the new German Empire. It was not nationalistic in the sense of wishing to expand German territory in Europe.

If Bismarck's aim after 1871 was to maintain the peace of Europe, his way of going about it was certainly not peaceable. He was used to constantly plotting and tricking and bluffing and bargaining, and this is what he continued to do. He wanted Germany (and himself in particular) to be at the centre of events, and he would stir things up so that he could use his diplomatic skills to gain some advantage. It might be claimed that his policy was nationalistic also in the sense of wishing to demonstrate the power and influence of the new Germany (although he sometimes preferred to manipulate others rather than let Germany make direct demands). He thought that tensions between the Great Powers were natural and that it was naive to suggest that they could be eliminated. What he tried to do was to balance the tensions to protect the German Empire. This meant that he was constantly stirring the pot and making new treaties and secret agreements. It is doubtful whether this was really the best way in the long run to protect Germany.

Maintaining a balance of tensions in Europe

Bismarck's first attempt to keep the peace between Germany, Austria–Hungary and Russia was the Dreikaiserbund (League of the Three Emperors) in 1873. Although this was a vague and informal agreement, which stressed the need for monarchs to work together against forces hostile to monarchy, it did not last long.

Russia's relations with Bismarck were shaken by his sabre-rattling against France in the 'War in sight' crisis in 1875. Later in 1875 there began a series of risings against Turkish rule in the Balkans, which opened up the possibility of Russia and Austria–Hungary taking territory there. They were almost at each other's throats in case one should get a larger share. Bismarck said that German interests in the Balkans 'were not worth the healthy bones of a single Pomeranian musketeer'. Therefore, he was pleased when in January 1877 Austria–Hungary agreed to stand aside if Russia attacked Turkey in return for a promise that Russia would not set up a large Slav state in the Balkans. He encouraged Russia to attack Turkey in April 1877, thinking that this would keep Russia occupied for some time and would weaken her enough to make her less demanding. In fact the threat of war between Austria–Hungary and Russia was not averted for long.

Russia did surprisingly well in the war against Turkey and in March 1878 imposed the Treaty of San Stefano on Turkey. Although Russia herself did not gain much Turkish territory, Bulgaria was to become independent from Turkey and was greatly expanded. There was evidence that Bulgaria would be dominated by Russia. Tsar Alexander II issued this proclamation:

> 'Russia is called by the decrees of Providence to pacify and conciliate all races and religions in Bulgaria . . . We have the firm intention of developing order and law in regions where there is now disorder.'

Austria–Hungary was horrified that Russia seemed likely to dominate such a large area as the new Bulgaria (contrary to their agreement) and insisted that the Treaty of San Stefano should be overturned. Bismarck believed he had to act to keep the peace and a congress was held in the German capital in June 1878. The Congress of Berlin was the most important international conference for twenty years. All the important statesmen of Europe attended, as can be seen in Figure 5.2.

Fig 5.2   Bismarck at the Congress of Berlin in 1878.

It was a glittering occasion which brought prestige to Germany as the host country. However, on this occasion Bismarck did not wish to appear to be throwing his weight about. He said to the Reichstag before the congress:

> 'I do not see peace negotiations as a situation in which we play the arbitrator and say: it shall be thus, and it is backed by the might of the German Empire, but I imagine a more modest role – more that of an honest broker, who really intends to do business.'

His main aim was to keep on good terms with both Austria–Hungary and Russia. This was no easy task, and even his diplomatic skill was not sufficient to bring it off. As Britain supported Austria, it was clear that Russia would have to make concessions. To try to end up on good terms with both sides Bismarck often appeared to be supporting the Russians. However, Russia greatly resented the outcome, which was that the new Bulgaria was much reduced in size and was not fully independent of Turkey. The Russians felt they had been robbed of the rewards of their successful war and blamed not only Austria and Britain, but also Bismarck as the organiser of the congress and as (they felt) a very lukewarm friend.

In 1879 Bismarck even more obviously failed to maintain the balance of tensions in Europe, and on this occasion there were serious long-term consequences. The traditional view of Bismarck was of a statesman who had a long-term plan (first for making and then for defending the German Empire) and who kept to it. In fact there is more evidence that he was so conscious of his skill in diplomatic tactics that he would stir up trouble in the hope of turning it to his advantage. In addition, he was far from being a cool master of the diplomatic chessboard. He was emotional and sometimes vindictive. For example, he never forgave the Russian chancellor Gortschakov for the snub he had given Bismarck in the 'War in sight' crisis in 1875. This may be one reason why he stirred up trouble with Russia in the early months of 1879. Perhaps he was irritated by the Russian reaction to the Congress of Berlin. Whatever the motivation, he was soon alarmed by the resulting Russian hostility and was looking for extra protection for Germany against Russia. In September 1879 he wrote to the king of Bavaria:

'I cannot resist the conviction that in the future, perhaps even in the near future, the peace is threatened by Russia and Russia alone . . . Austria feels just as ill at ease in view of the restlessness of Russian politics as we do, and she seems inclined to come to an understanding with us for the purpose of jointly resisting any Russian attack against either of us.

I should consider it as an essential guarantee of the peace of Europe and of Germany's safety, if the German Empire entered into such an agreement with Austria which would have for its object, now as before, carefully to cultivate the peace with Russia, yet to assist each other if, nevertheless, either of the two powers were to be attacked. In possession of such a mutual assurance both empires could, now as before, devote themselves to the renewed consolidation of the Three Emperors' Alliance.'

The result was a formal but secret alliance between Austria–Hungary and Germany in October 1879, which became known as the Dual Alliance. Each would support the other if attacked by Russia. Bismarck seems to have regarded this as another manoeuvre to protect Germany in a temporary difficulty (of his making) and not as a final choice by Germany between Austria and Russia. As he had suggested in his letter to the king of Bavaria, he did now seek to re-establish the alliance between the three empires and this was duly done in June 1881.

The new Dreikaiserbund was another secret treaty in which the three agreed there would be no changes in the Balkans without their mutual agreement and that Russia should be allowed to expand in the eastern part of the Balkans and Austria in the western part. However, Germany could no longer really claim to be even-handed between Russia and Austria. Russia knew that Germany and Austria had an alliance against her. Bismarck actually compounded the fault by expanding it into a Triple Alliance in 1882 to include Italy. He may have thought that these were all temporary agreements to meet immediate problems. However, as it turned out, the Triple Alliance became a fixed part of Germany's policy. It was renewed again and again and carried the German and Austro–Hungarian Empires to their doom in the First World War.

In the short term the network of alliances which Bismarck had created between 1879 and 1882 appeared to work. However, by the mid-1880s Austria and Russia were again at odds as a result of renewed tension in the Balkans. War broke out between Bulgaria (which always looked to Russia for support) and Serbia (which looked to Austria). Only Austrian threats prevented Bulgaria from over-running Serbia. Russia and Austria were now unwilling to be together in even the vaguest alliance, and the Dreikaiserbund collapsed.

It might seem that Bismarck's juggling act had finally failed, that Germany could no longer hope to be on good terms with both Austria and Russia, and that Russia was now likely to make an agreement with France and encircle Germany in the way that he had always feared. It was characteristic of Bismarck that he in no way accepted defeat and that, in this dangerous situation, his policy reached new heights of complexity and falsehood.

If there could no longer be an alliance of Germany, Austria–Hungary and Russia, Bismarck could have separate alliances with Austria and Russia. He therefore agreed to the 'Reinsurance Treaty' with Russia in June 1887. Under this Russia would be allowed if she wished to seize the Straits and Constantinople (held by Turkey) to prevent warships of other countries passing through into the Black Sea. This was directly contrary to a provision of the Dual Alliance. If it were ever carried out or if it even became public, Bismarck would be in serious trouble with Austria. He therefore made sure that he would never have to fulfil the promise to Russia by encouraging an agreement between Austria, Italy and

Britain in December 1887 to keep the Straits open. Russia would never defy the British navy, and so Bismarck's agreement with Russia would never have to be implemented.

Bismarck's policy in the late 1880s was, of course, completely dishonest. However, peace was maintained and in Bismarck's time Russia and France never came together to encircle Germany. It has been argued that Bismarck's successful exercise of power politics, both in the unification of Germany and in its defence in the 1870s and 1880s, led Germans to think that a great statesman had to be unscrupulous and dishonest. This, it has been claimed, made them more willing to accept Hitler. However, it is doubtful whether Bismarck's foreign policy really was successful as long as he was in power. There is plenty of evidence that by the late 1880s no European statesman trusted him any longer. In 1887 even the foreign minister of his firmest ally, Austria–Hungary, wrote that his attitude to Turkey:

> 'causes confusion and distrust . . . What will the Turks make of this, and is it to be wondered at if they conclude that reliable alliances are no longer to be had? It must be because of the very vulnerable position of Germany between France and Russia that Bismarck keeps trying to separate Russia from France by showing favour to the Emperor Alexander in the Balkans.'

However, no sooner had Bismarck concluded the Reinsurance Treaty with Russia in 1887 than he was whipping up anti-Russian feeling in Germany in order to persuade the Reichstag to grant taxes for the army for another seven years. Thus it is unlikely that the Russians trusted Bismarck any longer after the Reinsurance treaty, and highly probable that they were moving towards an alliance with France even before Bismarck was dismissed in 1890. The old juggler's clubs really were falling round him as he left the stage.

Bismarck and imperialism

In the 1870s Bismarck had no interest in acquiring colonies for Germany outside Europe and he was happy to leave this to Britain and France. He said at this time that 'a colonial policy for us would be just like the silk fur coats of Polish noblemen who have no shirts'. Colonies were a luxury which Germany could not afford. In any case there were more pressing matters to occupy his attention. As he once put it to an explorer who was trying to interest him in Africa, 'My map of Africa lies in Europe. Here is Russia and here is France and we are in the middle; that is my map of Africa.' In the late 1870s and early 1880s he became more willing to help German merchants who were being prevented from selling their goods in distant places by the forces of their rivals. However, in 1884 it was still possible for a cartoon to be

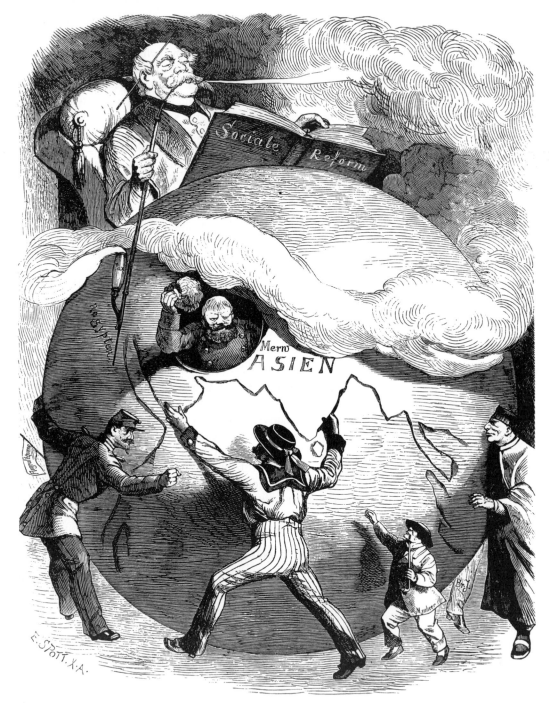

Fig 5.3 *Bismarck was interested in social reform while other European powers collected colonies.*

published suggesting that he was more interested in social reform at home than in collecting colonies (see Figure 5.3).

It was therefore a considerable surprise at the time, and has puzzled historians ever since, that in 1884 and 1885 Bismarck at last set out to gather colonies. In these two years Germany acquired several territories in Africa (German East Africa, Cameroon, Togoland, and South-West Africa) and some islands in the Pacific Ocean. This is how he explained his colonial policy to the Reichstag in June 1884:

> 'It would not be right for us to occupy tracts of land where we have no interests merely to encourage German emigration, have the area controlled by German officials and erect garrisons there. We do not possess properly trained officials for this purpose; that would be too expensive for us and would strain our navy too much... It is something else again to place under the protection of the Reich the free settlements of citizens of the Reich in areas which are not under the recognised rule of other nations. I hold it to be a duty of the Reich to place under her protection such settlements overseas by citizens of the Reich, not only their trading posts, but also the territory acquired by them.'

In various European countries in the 1880s (including Germany), 'Imperialists' were arguing that their countries needed colonies to show their national greatness and to find a living for their surplus population. Bismarck's speech shows that he did not take this view. He wanted to place under German rule and protection places where German merchants had settled and which were not already held by other European powers. Important merchants in Bremen and Hamburg had been pressing him to do this. The territories round these places would also become German, which would ensure that people there bought German goods. German industry was expanding rapidly and, since Bismarck had raised the customs dues on foreign goods coming into Germany in 1879, Germans could not expect their goods to be allowed freely into the colonies of other countries. There were, therefore, strong economic reasons for having colonies. In addition in 1884 and early 1885 there was a brief period when Germany was on good terms with Russia, with Austria–Hungary, and even (for a time) with France. Germany was in a strong position, therefore, to claim colonies and Bismarck always had an eye for an opportunity. On the other hand, Britain feared that her colonies in Africa would be threatened. This sowed the seeds in British public opinion of a new suspicion of German policy, which in time was to have serious consequences.

William II and Weltpolitik, 1890–1914

In 1914 William II led Germany into the First World War, which ended with over two million Germans dead, the collapse of the German Empire, and the loss of some of its European lands and of all its colonies. The result was the establishment of a weak republic which paved the way for Hitler's dictatorship and a Second World War which damaged Germany even more than the First World War had done. There is, therefore, general agreement that William II's 'Weltpolitik' (world policy) was a failure. The questions asked by historians are what he was trying to do, and why it went so badly wrong. These are the principal issues you should think about:

1. How far did William II follow an aggressive foreign policy to satisfy a German longing for national greatness which Bismarck had encouraged by building up the German Empire, but had failed to satisfy by his complicated balancing act designed to protect it? In other words, how far was nationalism the driving force of William's policy?

2. How far was his policy designed to solve economic and social problems at home – for example, the need to find markets for German industry which was expanding more rapidly than any of its rivals; and the need to use foreign adventures to distract attention from the growing threat by industrial workers to the way Germany was ruled?

3. In 1914 did the German government deliberately use the murder of the Austrian Emperor's heir as an excuse to start a war in the hope that it would establish Germany as a world power and that it would protect the power of the existing rulers of Germany?

These issues raise questions about *authority* in Germany and among the nations of Europe, and about the *ideology* and sense of *identity* of different groups of people in Germany.

TASK

Work in groups.

Think about some German soldiers discussing at the end of the First World War in November 1918 what had gone wrong. They are now thinking about German foreign policy between 1890 and the outbreak of war in 1914 and remembering what they had thought about it before the war.

One or two members in each group can take the part of one of these soldiers (but choose a different one from the one whose views you researched in Issue 4).

Number One is the son of a Prussian landowner. He was already an army officer before the First World War began. He very much admired the Emperor then, and believed that Germany's national greatness made it necessary to build up her army and navy.

Number Two is the son of the owner of a coalmine in the Rhineland. He was a university student before the war began. Like his father, he thought then that German industry depended on a large army and navy

and that the workers should be kept in their place.

Number Three worked in an engineering works in Berlin. He was a local organiser for his trade union and for the Social Democratic Party. Before the war he believed that the workers should have a greater say in how Germany was ruled, and should be given better pay and living and working conditions. He thought that money should be spent on this rather than on building up the army and navy. He only supported the war after it seemed in August 1914 that Germany had been attacked by Russia.

Make notes on what your character would have thought at the outbreak of war, and what he thinks now at the end of the war about German foreign policy between 1890 and 1914.

Explain your point of view to the other members of the group. And make notes on the points of view of the other members of the group.

The origins of Weltpolitik

From the outset William II had a strong sense of Germany's national greatness and it is possible to argue that this was the reason for his first foreign policy decision – not to renew the Reinsurance Treaty with Russia in 1890. Perhaps his view was that Germany was too powerful to need the kind of undignified double-dealing implied by this treaty. In addition, his advisers also argued that it was too dangerous to continue contradictory commitments. They persuaded him that Germany would do better to seek an arrangement with Britain. With this in mind, the new German government agreed in 1890 to a carving up of land in Africa which did not suggest that it was keen to build up its empire, but was, on the contrary, very generous to Britain.

In the event, Britain was not in the least interested in an alliance with Germany, and Russia moved rapidly towards an agreement with France, which was completed in 1894. France and Russia were now committed to supporting each other if either should be attacked by Germany. As a result Germany faced the prospect of a war on two fronts – just what Bismarck had struggled to prevent, and which (as a result of this agreement) began in due course in 1914.

The foreign policy of William's government in the early 1890s was obviously very unsuccessful. It is not fair to put it down simply to a foolhardy belief in Germany's greatness, stripped of Bismarck's caution and his understanding of the dangers facing the new empire. This policy attempted to be more sophisticated than that. On the other hand, William's own personality was undoubtedly an important factor in its failure. We have seen that he often changed his mind (depending on which advisers were in favour at the moment), and he did not work hard enough to develop his own detailed understanding of politics. A recent writer, Jurgen Tampke, has described William in this way:

'He was not a good statesman, judged on any standard; in fact he must rank as one of the least-talented rulers of his age. He never really understood that the German Empire was a relatively young nation and in many ways still very fragile and vulnerable to internal crises, nor did he ever comprehend the subtleties of international relations.'

(*Twentieth-Century Germany: Quest for Power*)

William's lack of understanding is shown very clearly by remarks he made in 1892 on one of his frequent cruises on the royal yacht:

'I hope Europe will gradually come to realise the fundamental principle of my policy: leadership in the peaceful sense – a sort of Napoleonic supremacy – a policy which gave expression to its ideas by force of arms – in the peaceful sense. I am of the opinion that it is already a success that I, having come to govern at so early an age, stand at the head of German armed might yet have left my sword in its scabbard and have given up Bismarck's policy of eternally causing disruption, to replace it with a peaceful foreign situation such as we have not known for many years.'

In these remarks he appears to believe his policy is one of peace, but compares himself with Napoleon, who was constantly at war.

By 1893 William's policy was (much too late) to seek a new agreement with Russia, while keeping open the possibility of Britain joining the Triple Alliance.

As people at home were now becoming puzzled by the lack of success or of direction of German policy in Europe, William's government increasingly tried to make its presence felt in the colonies. Inevitably this caused friction with Britain, which had the largest empire, and this friction was increased by the threatening tone of the emperor's personal interventions. The classic example of this occurred in 1896. The British authorities in South Africa were trying to expand their control and in late 1895 a raid was made into the republic of Transvaal (ruled by Boers, the descendants of Dutch settlers). When the raid failed, William II sent this telegram to President Kruger of the Transvaal:

> 'I express to you my sincere congratulations that, supported by your people and without calling for help from friendly powers, you have succeeded by your energetic action against armed bands that invaded your country as disturbers of the peace, and have therefore been able to restore peace and safeguard the independence of the country from outside attacks.'

The British were extremely angry at what seemed to them to be interference in matters which did not concern Germany, and they were particularly irritated by the implication that on another occasion Germany would be willing to help the Boers. The British government felt increasingly suspicious about German motives, and British public opinion began to become hostile to Germany. The new popular newspapers carried anti-German articles, and the windows of German shops in Britain were smashed. This suspicion and this hostility were to have serious consequences later.

However, these moves by Germany were more than an attempt to distract attention from an unsuccessful policy in Europe and more than the tactless comments of an erratic emperor. They reflected the views of an important and growing section of German public opinion, and to many they seemed necessary to meet Germany's vital economic interests. Pressure groups like the Pan-German League and the Colonial Union campaigned for Germany to join more fully in the race of the European powers for colonies. These campaigns channelled the nationalistic feelings of a large number of Germans in all social classes in the 1890s. They felt that both Germany's traditions and what she had achieved in recent generations (a unified homeland, a rapidly growing population and economy, and a large and well-equipped national army) entitled Germany to expect that her greatness should be more generally recognised. These ambitions were not fulfilled by Bismarck's foreign policy which (although active) was basically defensive; nor were they fulfilled by Germany's reluctance to acquire overseas colonies. Figures 5.4 and 5.5 are cartoons which show in a humorous way the qualities which the Germans thought made them particularly well equipped to rule colonies.

These nationalistic ambitions were encouraged by German businessmen. As we have seen on page 83, business and industry were growing faster in Germany in the 1890s than in any other European country. German businessmen needed new markets in which to sell the goods streaming from their factories and new ventures in which to invest their profits. Of course they could sell to and invest in places which were not under German rule, and

Lieutenant von Strehlau, frisch zur Schutztruppe in Afrika angekommen: „Nette Gegend soweit! —

Da muss Ordnung rin!"

*Fig 5.4 and Fig 5.5
Cartoons showing an
African colony before
and after the arrival of
the Germans (1896).*

they had set up branches of their firms as well as German banks in China, South Africa and Latin America. Figure 5.6 is a cartoon published in 1900. It shows a wedding in Cairo at which the Egyptians (whose country was controlled by Britain) are laden with German chocolates and wine.

However, German businessmen felt that their prospects would be better if at least some of the places they sold to could be under German rule. They also wanted a bigger German navy. Building the ships would give profitable orders to their firms and the fleet would then protect the merchant ships which carried their goods around the world. All these pressures reinforced William II's government's wish and political need to cut more of a dash in the world. A famous statement of the government's view was made in 1897 by Bernhard von Bülow (then foreign secretary and two years later to become chancellor). In a Reichstag debate he

Fig 5.6   A cartoon of a wedding in Cairo.

answered some members who were nervous about getting involved in rivalries with the empires of other European powers around the world. He said:

'Fears have been expressed that we are about to enter into a risky venture. Don't you worry, gentlemen. Neither the Chancellor nor his advisers are the kind of people that seek unnecessary conflict. We don't all feel the necessity to put our fingers in every pie. However, we do hold the opinion that it is not advisable to exclude Germany at the very beginning from the competitions of other countries. [Cries of 'Bravo'.]

The times when the Germans left the earth to the influence of one of their neighbours, the seas to another – these times are over. We see it as one of our most prominent tasks to support the interests of our ships, our trade and our industries, particularly in East Asia. We must demand that German missionaries, German goods, the German flag and German ships are treated with as much respect in China as those of other powers. [Lively cries of 'Bravo'.] We are only too happy to allow for the interest of other nations in East Asia provided that our own interests are treated with the same respect. ['Bravo'.] In a word, we don't want to put anyone in the shadow, but we also demand a place under the sun.'

This policy of demanding 'a place under the sun' became a major feature of German foreign policy from the late 1890s. It was now that the term 'Weltpolitik' (world policy) came to be generally used. Some historians have suggested that from the outset it was really a trick to distract German workers from demanding better pay and conditions and more political rights by entertaining them with foreign adventures. Leading German politicians, military men and businessmen certainly saw this as one of its advantages. For example, shortly after Bülow became foreign secretary in 1897, he wrote that 'only a successful foreign policy can help to reconcile, pacify, rally, unite.' On the other hand, when he became chancellor in 1899, his government tried to win the support of the workers by improved welfare benefits. In any case, as we have seen, there were many motives behind Weltpolitik. It was the property of more than one interest group and it won support among Germans of all classes and of many political views.

Accelerating rivalries

As the role of Weltpolitik required, Germany played an increasingly active role on the colonial stage from the late 1890s. Bülow's 'place under the sun' speech in 1897 made particular reference to East Asia. Later that year Germany acquired Kiaochow as a base on the coast of China. Figure 5.7 is a cartoon of 1899 about German ambitions in China. China is being invited to join the 'German club'.

It is significant that the naval officer who surveyed the Chinese coast and recommended the site of the German base was Alfred von Tirpitz. Weltpolitik depended on an increase in German naval power, and in 1898 Tirpitz became secretary for the navy. In close co-operation with Bülow, he set about expanding the German fleet. Navy laws were passed by the Reichstag in 1898 and 1900 granting the money for the building of new ships. The 1900 navy law was particularly frank about its purpose:

'For the German Empire of today, the security of its economic development, and especially of its world trade, is a life question. For this purpose the German Empire needs not only peace on land but also peace at sea – not, however, peace at any

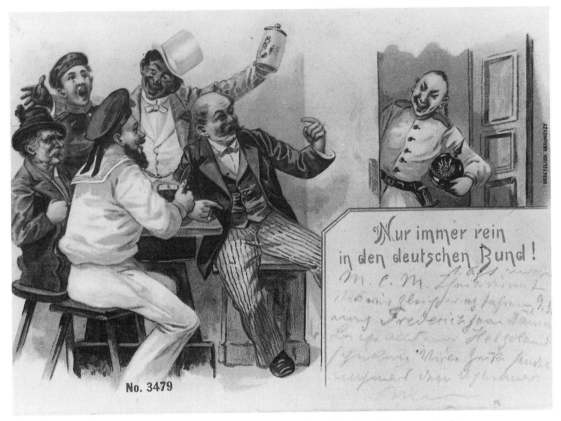

No. 3479

Nur immer rein in den deutschen Bund!

Fig 5.7   A cartoon showing China being invited to join the 'German club'.

price, but peace with honour, which satisfies Germany's just requirements.

To protect Germany's sea trade and colonies there is only one means – Germany must have a fleet so strong that even for the adversary with the greatest sea power a war against it would involve such dangers as to imperil his position in the world.'

The 'greatest sea power' was Britain, and this law was directed against her. It provided for the building not only of cruisers for the protection of merchant ships, but also of a fleet of battleships which could give the British battleships a good fight if required. Although this was claimed to be defensive, Britain rightly saw it as a deliberate threat to her naval supremacy, which had been unquestioned since the days of Nelson a century before. There was a enormous feeling of national pride in Germany as the ships of the new fleet were launched (and not just from the businessmen who had campaigned for the Reichstag to pass the navy laws).

British suspicion of German motives was greatly increased, and in 1904 Britain made the 'Entente Cordiale' (Friendly agreement) with France. Strictly speaking, this was only a settlement of colonial differences. However, it was significant that Britain wanted to get on better terms with France. France certainly hoped that ultimately Britain would help her against Germany, and even in the short term she did get some diplomatic support.

In 1905 Germany, in pursuit of her Weltpolitik, tried to humiliate France by reducing her influence in the north African state of Morocco. During one of his cruises William II called on the Sultan of Morocco at Tangiers. These comments of his give some idea of the sort of offence which the policy caused (and of William's particular gift for insult). When the French representative to the Sultan's court welcomed the emperor to Morocco he replied that:

> 'The visit of the All Highest means that His Majesty demands free trade for Germany and complete equality with other nations. His Majesty remarked that he would come to an understanding with the Sultan as a free and equal ruler of an independent country, that His Majesty himself would know how to bring all his influence to achieve his rightful claims and expected that this would be respected also by France. The French representative went pale, wanted to reply, but, prevented by a curt dismissal, left with his head lowered.'

An international conference was held in 1906 to deal with the Moroccan question, and Britain helped France to rebuff Germany. Meantime naval rivalry between Germany and Britain reached new heights as they strove to re-equip their fleets with a new and more powerful class of battleship, the 'Dreadnought'. Figures 5.8 and 5.9 show how alarming the German fleet seemed in Britain. They were published in a popular magazine, *The Sphere*, in 1908 and show a caricature of the German naval flag and a very threatening drawing of the first German 'Dreadnought'.

In 1907 Britain made an 'Entente' with Russia of the sort which she had already made with France. The German government began to complain that it was being 'encircled' by potential enemies. It is true that Germany was now becoming isolated in Europe in the way that Bismarck had feared, with the two greatest land powers, France and Russia, ranged against her (possibly to be helped by the greatest naval power, Britain). On Germany's side was only the decaying Austro–Hungarian Empire, with the limited (and uncertain) help of Italy. In part the German government had provoked this by its aggressive and nationalistic policy.

Another example of this was its behaviour in the Second Moroccan Crisis in 1911. The German foreign secretary, Kiderlen, thought he could weaken the Entente Cordiale by exploiting the disorders France was facing in Morocco. However, he overplayed his hand by sending the German gunboat *Panther* to the Moroccan port of Agadir. The result was an international crisis in which Britain became even more closely linked to France.

THE KAISER'S NAVY.

Drawn, from details at present available, by A. B. Cull

THE FIRST OF GERMANY'S "DREADNOUGHTS"—THE "NASSAU," LAUNCHED AT WILHELMSHAVEN ON MARCH 7

Fig 5.8 and Fig 5.9 The German navy as seen from London, 1908.

Behind the German posturing there were serious issues at stake. We have examined the economic, colonial and and naval rivalry which divided Germany and Britain. There were also serious economic issues at stake between Germany and Russia.

We have seen that the Prussian junkers played a very important part in running the German Empire and the German army. Their financial position depended on the grain production of their estates, which were mostly east of the River Elbe. These 'East Elbians' were threatened about 1900 by the import of grain from the United States and Russia. The East Elbian landowners were such a powerful force in Germany that they were able to ensure that their interests were protected. In return for helping the businessmen in the Reichstag to pass the navy law in 1900, they were able to have a law passed in 1902 which increased customs duties so much on grain coming from Russia that it was effectively kept out. Russian landowners, who might otherwise have felt that they had much in common with the Prussian junkers, suffered badly. Ill-feeling between Germany and Russia was also increased by economic rivalry in the Balkans, Turkey and Persia. German and Russian firms were both trying to increase their markets in these areas (with the more efficient Germans getting the lion's share). As in other areas, economic and political rivalries became entangled. In 1908 Russia was outraged when Austria–Hungary annexed the Balkan states of Bosnia and Herzegovina. As we have seen on page 94, the Russians and Austrians had been rivals in that area for many years. However, Germany backed Austria, not only as her partner in the Triple Alliance, but also because of her wish to win more business orders there than the Russians.

The outbreak of the First World War

In the aftermath of the First World War, the victors were very clear that Germany had been responsible for the war. The peace treaty stated:

> 'The Allied governments affirm, and Germany accepts, the responsibility of Germany and her allies for causing all the loss and damage to which the Allied governments and their peoples have been subjected as a result of the war.'

It seemed later that this was an attempt to blame others for the terrible loss of life and that the truth was that the responsibility was not so clear-cut.

In the 1950s and 1960s most historians believed that the First World War occurred because the complicated system of alliances and agreements in Europe had got out of control. The accelerating rivalries between the powers led to a series of crises (some of which you have just read about in this chapter). The events of 1914, it was thought, began as another of these crises. The Archduke Franz Ferdinand (the heir to the Austrian throne) was murdered at Sarajevo in Bosnia on 28 June 1914 by young Serbian extremists. Although Bosnia was ruled by Austria, the Bosnians were of the same Slav race as the Serbs. The Austrians decided to take their revenge on Serbia. However, Serbia was backed by another Slav country – Russia. The machinery of the alliances now began turning and propelled Europe towards a general war which nobody particularly wanted. By a series of accidents (for which no one in particular was to blame), this crisis was not efficiently managed, as the previous ones had been, and Europe slipped into war. This in general terms was the view taken by David Thomson, writing in 1957:

> 'Berchtold [the Austrian chancellor] lit the fuse when no one had time to extinguish it. From that decisive act everything else followed. Russia ordered general mobilisation on 30th July, Germany on 31st July; and Germany declared war against Russia on 1st August, against France on 3rd August. Germany's ultimatum to Belgium on 3rd August, and its rejection as being a violation of Belgian neutrality, ensured Britain's entry into the war the following day. The bonds of the alliances held firm, and the two armed camps clashed in open battle at last.'

This was a very convenient view at a time when the western powers were building the Federal Republic of Germany into an important part of their cold war alliance against Russia.

It is interesting that it was a German historian, Fritz Fischer, who did the most to demolish that interpretation. He did it by uncovering a large number of documents which most historians would now agree show that it was the fault of the German leaders that the crisis of 1914 led to a general war. He showed that some of them were even hoping for war two years earlier. On 8 December 1912 William II met his top military and naval advisers. One of them wrote this record of what was said:

> 'General von Moltke (Chief of the Army General Staff): I believe a war is unavoidable. But we ought to do more through the press to encourage the popularity of a war against Russia.
>
> The Emperor supported this and told the State secretary (Tirpitz) to use his press contacts too to work in this direction. Tirpitz said that the navy would prefer to see the postponement of the great fight for one and a half years. Moltke said the navy would not be ready even then and the army would get into an increasingly unfavourable position, for the enemies were arming more strongly than we, as we were very short of money.
>
> In the afternoon I wrote to the Reich Chancellor about the influencing of the press.'

It is striking that the civilian leaders of the government were not present at this meeting and were merely informed of the result. However, throughout the life of the German empire the monarch was entitled to arrange matters of war and peace without reference to his civilian ministers. It was only Bismarck's personality which ensured that this had never happened before 1890.

Another example of the supremacy of the military in decision-making (which was to be very relevant in the outbreak of war) was the Schlieffen Plan. In 1900 Alfred von Schlieffen, the chief of the German General Staff, informed the government that in the event of a two-front war the army did not intend to be bound by international agreements. By 1905 a plan had been adopted for the army to defeat France quickly in the west (by invading through Belgium) in order then to concentrate its strength in the east against Russia. Bülow raised no objection, although invading Belgium would be both contrary to Germany's treaty commitments and threatening to Britain, which lay a short distance away across the English Channel. This was an ominous precedent for the fateful decisions which were soon to be made.

There were external and internal reasons why important sections of the German leadership would want a European war sometime after 1912. We have seen that Germany's nationalistic and clumsy foreign policy had resulted in isolating her from the most powerful states in Europe. France and Russia were now arming fast and seemed increasingly likely to be joined by Britain if there were a general war. The German generals believed that this made a war inevitable and that, if it did not happen soon, their enemies would have overtaken them in the size of their forces and in the quality of their weapons.

Within Germany, you will remember that in 1912 the power of the trade unions was growing fast and that in that year the Social Democratic Party (SPD) became the largest party in the Reichstag. This made it extremely difficult for a majority in the Reichstag to be obtained by the alliance of the Prussian landowners and the traditionally-minded businessmen who helped the emperor to run Germany. They could have made a deal with the industrial workers whom the SPD represented. They could have given the workers a larger say in running the country, and better pay and living and working conditions. As we have seen in Issue 4 (page 87), they were not prepared to pay the price. Since they would not make concessions to the trades unions and to the SPD, they had to find some other way out. For many of the traditional rulers of Germany, the answer was a general war. They thought that it should take place soon for military reasons and they believed that it would also remove the threat posed by the trade unions and SPD to the traditional way in which the businesses and government of Germany were run. The workers would be caught up in the great national struggle. They would be won over by the nationalistic enthusiasm of a country fighting for its existence. They would realise that their own interests were less important than those of the nation as a whole. Whether they were in the armed forces or in the factories they would once again be willing to obey their superiors in the traditional way.

Fischer has argued that these were the reasons why important sections of the leadership of Germany wanted war even before 1914:

'The aim was to consolidate the position of the ruling class with a successful imperialist foreign policy; indeed it was hoped a war would resolve the growing social tensions. By involving the masses in the great struggle those parts of the nation which had hitherto stood apart would be integrated into the monarchical state. By 1912 at any rate the domestic crisis was apparent. The decision to go to war was, in addition to the domestic consideration, based above all on military reflections, which in turn depended on economic and political objectives.'

Fischer has found a great deal of evidence to show that in 1914, during the five weeks between the murder of the Archduke Franz Ferdinand and the outbreak of war, German military leaders were doing everything they could to bring about war and to get their forces into the field first. This does not mean that everyone in Berlin wanted war. But the emperor seems to have thought that the crisis gave Germany the opportunity of humiliating her enemies and of breaking out of her 'encirclement'. He hoped that her enemies would give in to German threats and that war would be avoided. If they did not give way, it would be better to have a war now than later. The chancellor, Bethmann-Hollweg, was conscious of the dangers to Germany of a general war, and he would have liked to localise the war to one between Austria and Serbia. However, as we have seen, in Germany matters of war and peace were not under civilian control. When it became clear in mid-July that the war would not be localised, the German generals took over control of policy. Bethmann-Hollweg's main contribution now seems to have been to make it appear that Germany had been attacked by Russia. Bethmann wrote on 28 July 1914 to the German ambassador in Vienna:

> 'According to the statements of the Austrian General Staff, an active military movement against Serbia will not be possible before 12th August. As a result, the German Government is placed in the extraordinarily difficult position of being exposed in the meantime to the conference proposals of other governments. If it continues to maintain its previous aloofness in the face of such proposals it will incur the odium of having been responsible for a world war. A successful war on three fronts cannot be commenced and carried on on any such basis. It is essential that the responsibility for the eventual extension of the war should fall on Russia.'

Bethmann managed to manoeuvre Russia into mobilising first. The trade unions and the SPD regarded the Russian government as a dyed-in-the-wool enemy of the workers. As a result, most of their members agreed to support the war. As one of the military leaders wrote, 'The mood is brilliant. The government has managed magnificently to appear the attacked party.'

Germany went to war in August 1914 in a mood of nationalistic enthusiasm. One newly commissioned officer said 'War is like

Fig 5.10 *Sedan Day in Berlin in 1914 with Russian and French guns being paraded through the streets.*

Christmas.' Figure 5.10 gives a feeling of the enthusiasm for the war. It shows captured Russian and French guns being paraded in Berlin in September 1914 on 'Sedan Day' – the anniversary of the great victory in 1870 which did so much to bring about the unification of Germany. Enthusiastic people line the Unter den Linden street and crowd on to the roofs of the public buildings.

Of course Paris, London, St Petersburg and Vienna saw similar scenes and heard the expression of similar sentiments. Nationalist views were popular throughout Europe in the early twentieth century. But German nationalism and German determination to be recognised as a world power played a larger part than the nationalistic feelings of any other country in bringing about the First World War. The Germans had more to prove than the longer established Great Powers. It is difficult to exaggerate the consequences of this – not only for Germany but also for the rest of the world.

ESSAY

Choose one of the following views about German foreign policy between 1871 and 1914, and write an essay to discuss it.

1. 'Bismarck's foreign and colonial policy was not aggressively nationalistic. He was really only interested in preserving what he had created up to 1871.'
2. 'The dishonesty of Bismarck's foreign policy after 1871 was not of great benefit to Germany's interests at the time and was a dangerous legacy for the future.'
3. 'Nationalism was the driving force of German foreign policy under William II in a way it had not been under Bismarck.'
4. 'The aggressive foreign policy of William II and Germany's entry to the First World War were mainly designed to protect the existing ruling class.'

The Weimar Republic

As late as the spring of 1918 Germany still had hopes of winning the First World War. In the east it had already been won. Russia had been knocked out of the war by the Bolshevik revolution in November 1917 and had been forced to agree to a humiliating peace treaty in March 1918. In the same month the German army launched the 'Victory Offensive' on the western front, which was designed to end the four years of bloody stalemate in the trenches and to enable Germany to score a knockout blow. It almost did so. The Germans twice made major breakthroughs, but did not have the manpower to follow them up. It soon became clear that the 'Victory Offensive' had in fact been the gambler's last throw. The British sea blockade was gradually wearing down Germany's ability to supply her forces and to feed her population. It had been hoped that unrestricted attacks by German submarines on all British merchant ships would bring Britain to her knees. What happened in fact was that it brought the United States of America into the alliance against Germany. American troops were flooding into France in the early months of 1918 and by July a million of them were reinforcing the French and British armies. As a result the allied counter-offensive in July was unstoppable. The German army did not collapse, but by the autumn it was retreating nearer and nearer to the German frontier. It became clear to the German 'war lords' (as they called themselves) and to the German people that the war had been lost.

In October 1918, the emperor appointed a new government, which for the first time was made answerable to the Reichstag as in other parliamentary democracies. It included representatives of the majority of the Social Democrat Party (SPD) which had fully supported the war effort. This was not intended as a just reward for their support. It had been recommended to William by the army leaders, Hindenburg and Ludendorff, in the hope of spreading the blame for the defeat they now knew was certain. However, events in Germany were soon spinning out of control of the emperor and of his new government.

At the beginning of November 1918 Germany was gripped by a combination of hardships because of food shortages, and because of demoralisation and confusion when people realised that the war had been lost. This was an explosive mixture of emotions, and a number of revolts soon occurred. The first was in the port of

Kiel, where the sailors rebelled on hearing that their admirals were thinking of taking the fleet to sea for a last stand against the British navy. Revolts soon became so widespread that it became clear that a revolution was under way. Meetings and demonstrations were held in favour of peace and reform. Many towns were taken over by bodies which called themselves (using the language of the Russian revolution) 'Workers' and Soldiers' Councils'. However, most of the German revolutionaries did not want (as the Russian Bolsheviks did) a workers' dictatorship. Most were not communists, but just wanted some form of democracy. In many cases the councils were influenced by the Independent Socialists. These were the minority of the Social Democrats who had opposed the war from the start and because of this had in 1916 broken away from the 'Majority Socialists' of the SPD. For example, on 7 November 1918 the state of Bavaria was declared a republic under an Independent Socialist leader. The Majority Socialists were afraid that they would be swept aside and they demanded that the emperor should abdicate in favour of one of his younger sons. William was in the relative safety of Spa in Belgium and could not be persuaded that his reign was over. Meantime signs that a revolt was brewing in Berlin persuaded the Majority Socialists that they had to act if they were to keep control. On 9 November one of their leaders, Scheidemann, went to the window of the Reichstag building and declared that Germany had become a republic. Figure 6.1 shows the large crowd which cheered his announcement.

An armistice was immediately agreed with the Allies to halt the fighting on the western front, and this came into force at 11 a.m. on 11 November (the time at which a minute's silence is still observed at church services held in Britain every year to remember our war dead).

What was claimed to be 'the war to end wars' had come to a close. With the war had ended the German Empire which had played so large a part in bringing it about. Despite the national pride it had aroused in so many Germans, the empire had lasted less than half a century. It was replaced by what became known as the 'Weimar Republic' because its inaugural meetings were held in Weimar. Weimar was a safe distance from the disorder and danger of Berlin. As the home of the great poet Goethe, it was also believed to represent the 'other Germany' – the Germany of culture rather than the Germany of aggression and militarism. In 1919 the new republic signed what most Germans regarded as a humiliating peace treaty with the Allies in the same Hall of Mirrors at Versailles where the German Empire had been proclaimed in 1871.

In the event, the Weimar Republic was even more short-lived than the German Empire. It 1933 it was swept aside by the 'Third Reich' of Hitler and the Nazi Party. The Nazis again gave Germany

Fig 6.1 The proclamation of the republic outside the Reichstag.

nationalistic and aggressive leadership and took her into the Second World War, which was even more destructive and humiliating for her than the First World War. The Nazis were also responsible for crimes against Jewish and other peoples which are so horrifying that they are beyond the ability of most people (including most Germans) fully to understand.

Historians have looked at the Weimar Republic to see if there was something fatally flawed about it which can explain the rise of the Nazis. This question can be divided into these issues:

1. Was the Weimar Republic doomed from the outset –
- because it left the army, the civil service, the law courts, schools and universities in the hands of men who had been appointed by the empire and continued to hanker after its aggressive and authoritarian ways?
- because it left the major industries of Germany (such as coal, steel and engineering) in the hands of the same owners who had always favoured an aggressive foreign policy to boost their profits and had shown themselves unwilling to work with trade unions to improve the conditions of their workers?
- because it was supported by too few political parties which actually believed in the republic? (This problem was worsened by the split between the Majority Socialists and the Independent Socialists during the revolution which set it up.)

- because it accepted the Versailles Peace Settlement? Most Germans believed that this settlement punished them unfairly, particularly in the high level of the 'reparations' Germany had to pay to make up the war losses of her former enemies. Did the burden of paying reparations cause the runaway inflation which in 1923 made the mark worthless, and with it destroyed the savings of many middle class Germans and ruined their confidence in the republic?

    Most Germans believed that the Versailles settlement prevented them (alone among European nations) from uniting all their people in one state. Did this create a deep nationalist ambition to continue the work of unification, which could not be met by the Weimar politicians, but only by some new aggressive party like the Nazis?

2. Alternatively, are these criticisms of the Weimar Republic based on hindsight, and are they unrealistic views of what it was practical in the circumstances for it to do? Was the Weimar Republic not establishing itself well in the late 1920s, with increased prosperity for most Germans, and with a golden age for writers, artists and architects? Could the republic not have survived (and could the Nazis not have remained a small party of extremists) had the great economic depression of 1929–32 not thrown everything off course?

These issues raise questions about the *authority* of the Weimar governments, the *ideology* of the political parties during the republic and the sense of *identity* of the Germans during this period.

TASK

Work in groups.

Some groups will collect evidence which suggests that the Weimar Republic was fatally flawed and that its failings were such that it was always likely to be replaced by some more authoritarian German state.

Other groups will collect evidence that the leaders of the Weimar Republic did as much as was possible in the circumstances, and that the republic was establishing itself well until it was hit by the world Depression in 1929.

Hold a class debate on the proposition that 'The Weimar Republic had fatal weaknesses and was bound to be replaced by a more aggressive and nationalistic German state.'

Listen carefully to and make notes on the arguments opposed to the ones which have been researched by your group.

A revolution which left the traditional leaders in charge

Some historians have argued that the revolution of 1918–19 was not sweeping enough and left too much power in the state and in business in the hands of the leading supporters of the empire. If only, they argue, the republican leaders had got rid of the army officers, the civil servants, the judges and the teachers left by the empire, and had taken into state ownership the leading coal, steel and engineering firms, then the republic would have been much stronger and the Nazis would have been unable to come to power. A clear explanation of this view has been given recently by Jurgen Tampke:

> 'Many historians today believe that the German November Revolution offered a genuine chance to alter existing inequalities, to lay the basis for a social and economic reconstruction of German society. Their argument is that the SPD leaders failed to realise the revolution's potential and were in part to blame for exposing the Republic to the political extremism which proved so fatal for Weimar Germany. Above all, the SPD should have remembered – in the light of the Empire's pre-war and wartime policies, which aimed at establishing German leadership in Europe – that it would be necessary to crush, or at least severely curtail, the power of the reactionary army establishment and of sections of German industry.'
>
> (*Twentieth-Century Germany: Quest for Power*)

Historians who take this view usually quote secret agreements made in the very early days of the republic between Majority Socialist (SPD) leaders on the one hand and representatives of the imperial army and of German industry on the other. These, they argue, show that the SPD leaders did not even try to remove many of the powerful men of imperial Germany.

One of these agreements was between Friedrich Ebert of the SPD and General Groener. Ebert was the leading member of the Council of People's Deputies or provisional government which ran the republic until its constitution was worked out in 1919, and then the president of the republic until his death in 1925. For many years he had been one of the most prominent members of the SPD and of the Majority Socialists, who supported the war. Only a day after the proclamation of the republic (that is, on 10 November 1918) General Groener set up a secret telephone link with Ebert and proposed an alliance between the army officers and the Majority

Socialists. This is how Groener later remembered it:

'The duty of the army command was now to lead the rest of the army speedily and in an orderly fashion . . . back into the homeland. It was also to enable the officer corps, as the bearer of the military tradition, to find its feet in the new situation . . .

The officer corps could, however, only co-operate with a government which took up the fight against radicalism and Bolshevism. Ebert accepted this, but he was in grave danger of losing control . . . What could be more logical than to offer Ebert – whom I knew to be an upright and reliable character and the most politically farsighted of his army of comrades – the support of the army and officer corps?

In the evening of 10th November I telephoned the Reich Chancellery and told Ebert that the army put itself at the disposal of the government, that in return for this the Field Marshall (Hindenburg) and the officer corps expected the support of the government in the maintenance of order and discipline in the army. The officer corps expected the government to fight against Bolshevism and was ready for the struggle. Ebert accepted my offer of an alliance. From then on we discussed the measures which were necessary every evening on a secret telephone line between the Reich Chancellery and the high command. The alliance proved successful.

We hoped through our action to gain a share of the power in the new state for the army and officer corps. If we succeeded, then we should have rescued into the new Germany the best and strongest elements of old Prussia, despite the revolution.'

This alliance can be used to suggest that Ebert sold out from the very start to the group of men who had run Germany under the emperor, and that from this stemmed the decisions to keep the old officer corps, civil servants, judges and teachers. However, Ebert and the Majority Socialists did not really desert their principles. Their main aim was to protect the parliamentary democracy which had already been set up in October 1918. They thought that changes in the way in which Germany was run and in the conditions of working people should come through the ballot box. With this in view they wanted the election as soon as possible of a national assembly which would decide the constitution of the republic. In the disorderly state of Germany in the aftermath of defeat, it would not be easy to organise fair elections. The government would need armed backing and Groener was offering this to it. In addition, there were extreme socialists (the 'Spartakists' led by Karl Liebknecht), who were campaigning, not for any form of democracy, but for a revolution on the model of the Russian Bolshevik revolution. This was contrary to the principles of Ebert and the Majority Socialists. In addition the Allied govern-ments were very afraid of 'Bolshevism', and Ebert feared that

Fig 6.2 Soldiers and sailors in Berlin during the early weeks of the 1918–19 revolution.

they would invade Germany if there were any sign that Bolshevism might get a grip there. To prevent this, he needed to be sure that he had the backing of the army.

Figure 6.2 shows a car full of soldiers and sailors at the Brandenburg gate in Berlin during the early weeks of the revolution. They are armed and flying the red flag. The red flag was copied from the Russian revolution and it was thought this meant that their aim was a people's dictatorship on the Russian model. Most historians now think that only a very few Germans wanted this in 1918. However, Germans who had supported the empire worried for a long time about the danger of a Bolshevik take over.

Another agreement which the critics of the Social Democrats complain of was between the major industrial firms, led by Hugo Stinnes, and the trade unions, led by the Social Democrat Carl Legien. In this case discussions had actually started before the empire collapsed. One of the employers' representatives described later what was done:

'The suggestion I made in July 1918 to some of the leaders of our industry to establish links with the trade unions before we were swept away by the flood of events, was accepted . . . Agreement was reached on the following points: recognition of the trade unions as the official representatives of the workers, the signing of wage agreements in the individual branches of industry and the dropping by the employers of "company unions" [which had been set up by employers to give the impression that they were dealing with trade unions when in reality they were not].

On 11th November (after the revolution) agreement was reached on an eight-hour day, but this was made acceptable to the employers by Legien agreeing that its introduction would be dependent on other countries accepting it also. On 15th November all the trade unions and employers' associations gave their approval to the agreement.

Thus we had prepared the ground for that co-operation which established order in the following few years. It is no exaggeration to say that this co-operation saved Germany from chaos and from Bolshevik revolution. What happened in all other revolutions, that the workers turned against the employers, did not happen here because the unions co-operated with the employers in the preservation of order.'

This alliance, like that between Ebert and Groener, can be used to suggest that in the industrial field also the Social Democrats sold out to the established order from the very start of the republic. What they should have been doing, it has been said, was to take some of the most important industries into state owner-ship and to get rid of the employers who had done so much to support the authoritarian policies of the empire at home and who had profited so much from its aggressive foreign policy. On the other hand, the Social Democrats got in November 1918 what they had been seeking for many years – the right of trade unions to organise freely in factories and to negotiate wages and con-ditions on behalf of their workers. They were also afraid that any attempt to take factories away from their owners would cause chaos and add to the hardship many people were already suffering. Figure 6.3 shows children whose parents had not been able to feed them queuing at a street soup kitchen in December 1918. They are well dressed, which shows that their families had not been poor for long. The Social Democrat trade union leaders did not want to do anything which might worsen the chaos in the economy at the time of Germany's defeat and cause even more suffering.

On the other hand, members of the local Workers' and Soldiers' Councils, although not Bolsheviks, wanted more reform than the Social Democrats were offering. They were supporters of the Independent Socialists, who had broken away from the SPD because they did not want to support the war. They did not want a workers' dictatorship on the Russian model. What they wanted was direct action now to remove the emperor's men from the army, from the civil service and from industry, and to create a socialist Germany. Elections could *then* be held for a national assembly. Its job would be to put the finishing touches to the

Fig 6.3   Children at a street soup kitchen in December 1918.

constitution of a Germany which they would have ensured would be free of the authoritarian figures of the empire, would be safe for democracy, and would have some of its industries owned by the people.

These Independent Socialists were to be found not only in the local Workers' and Soldiers' Councils – Ebert had been obliged to include three of them (together with three Majority Socialists) in the Council of People's Deputies which acted as the provisional government.

Historians who believe that the republic was compromised from the start say that Ebert should have accepted some of their policies and got rid of the imperial officers and civil servants. On the other hand, the Independent Socialists had no very clearly worked out plans for how exactly their policies could be carried out. Meantime Ebert had to keep the country running and prevent the chaos which he feared would cause a Spartakist or Bolshevik revolution and, as a result, an allied invasion of Germany. The only people he believed could do this were the servants of the imperial government. He justified this policy in a speech he made on 25 November 1918:

> 'We had to make sure, once we had taken over political power, that the Reich machine did not break down. We had to make sure the machine continued to operate so as to be able to maintain our food supplies and the economy. And that was not an easy task. We worked with all our strength day and night so as to prevent collapse and downfall within a few days. The six of us could not do that alone; we needed the experienced co-operation of experts. Had we removed the experienced heads of the Reich offices, had we replaced them with people who did

not possess the necessary knowledge and experience, then we should have faced failure in a few days. We therefore urgently appealed to all Reich officials to continue to exercise their duty until further notice.'

A historian who has defended Ebert is A. J. Nicholls. He believes that an attempt to use the Workers' and Soldiers' Councils to get rid of the old order could well have ended in a Russian-style dictatorship:

'It is certainly clear that socialist experiments could have seriously worsened Germany's already difficult economic situation and might well have led to civil war... With hindsight the majority Social Democrats were probably right to move as quickly as possible in the direction of parliamentary democracy. Germany was not Russia, and the German workers, let alone the middle class, would have been unlikely to tolerate a dictatorship... As it was, the constitution which resulted from Ebert's prudent leadership was certainly the most democratic in Germany's history, and would have been inconceivable had the monarchy survived...

Ebert and his Social Democrat colleagues were eager to re-establish order in Germany and to organise the election of a National Assembly. Once these objectives were gained it would be possible to negotiate a peace treaty and set about the reconstruction of Germany's economic life. They assumed that democratic elections would produce a very powerful socialist group in the new National Assembly. They had no reason to believe that the sort of Germany they wanted could not be created with the aid of existing officials.'

(*Weimar and the Rise of Hitler*)

However, for there to be a very powerful socialist group in the national assembly, the socialists had to remain reasonably united. The Social Democrats can be certainly be criticised for paying more attention to keeping the support of the servants of the old empire. They seemed less concerned to keep on good terms with the Independent Socialists who were members of the same government.

In December 1918 there was a dispute about the behaviour of the Independent Socialist police chief of Berlin, after which the Independent Socialists resigned from the government. When Ebert dismissed the police chief in January 1919, a rising was sparked off in Berlin. This is often called the 'Spartakist Rebellion' because it was joined by the Spartakist party, led by Karl Liebknecht and Rosa Luxemburg (who were murdered while the rising was being put down). However, it had not been started by the Spartakists, and it included various types of extreme socialists, including some Independent Socialists.

Ebert called in the 'Free Corps' to put down the rebels. These were former members of the imperial army, led by imperial officers and paid by supporters of the empire (including industrialists). They were only too happy to kill people they regarded as revolutionaries. However, the Independent Socialists never forgave the Social Democrats for using the Free Corps against some of their members. The socialists were now irretrievably divided, and this, as we shall see, weakened the prospects of the republic and in due course made it easier for Hitler to seize power.

A republic with too few friends

The first elections after the revolution were in January 1919 for the national assembly, which would frame the new constitution. The results seemed reasonably promising for the republic:

National assembly elections, January 1919

Party		Percentage of votes	Number of seats
USPD	(Independent Socialist)	7.6	22
SPD	(Social Democratic Party or 'Majority Socialists')	37.9	163
DDP	(Democratic Party – the old left-wing Liberals, who had split from the National Liberals in Bismarck's day)	18.6	75
Zentrum	(The mainly Catholic Centre Party)	19.7	91
DVP	(People's Party – the old National Liberals, mainly middle class, representing industry)	4.4	19
DNVP	(National People's Party – the old Conservatives, representing landowners, army officers, officials of the old empire)	10.3	44
Others		1.5	7

The three parties which supported the republic (SPD, DDP and Zentrum) won between them 76 per cent of the vote. At such an early stage in the republic's life, this seemed promising for its future. However, support for it did not continue to grow, but dropped instead. Armed risings against the republic occurred regularly for several years. In 1919 and 1920 there were risings by workers in Berlin and in other industrial areas, which were put down by the Free Corps or by the army. Those involved were disillusioned, because the government relied on the armed force of people who were really supporters of the old empire, and because the government was doing so little to make Germany a more socialist country. Their views were in most cases close to those of the Independent Socialists. (There was also a communist rising, quickly put down by the army, in 1921.)

In March 1920 there was a different sort of uprising. It was not by left-wing opponents of the republic, who wanted more socialism, but by right-wing opponents, who wanted a return to the empire. The 'Kapp Putsch' (or uprising) was led by Wolfgang Kapp, and supported by soldiers who were likely to be disbanded as a result of the Versailles peace settlement. When the putsch seemed about to succeed, the emperor (in exile in Holland) thought he would soon be home. However, it was defeated by a general strike of workers across the whole of Germany.

It was significant that the army, which was happy enough to put down workers' risings, refused to act against the Kapp Putsch. The commander-in-chief said that 'the army does not shoot upon the army.' It was also noted that only a few of the plotters were put on trial, and that only one light sentence was given – a general was retired on pension, although he could have been executed for high treason. This made it obvious that the generals and the judges were not really supporters of the republic.

In June 1920 a Reichstag election was held, and the results were significantly different from those of January 1919:

National assembly elections, January 1919 and Reichstag elections, June 1920

Party	Number of seats	
	January 1919	June 1920
USPD (Independent Socialist)	22	83
SPD (Majority Socialists)	163	103
DDP (Democratic Party)	75	39
Zentrum (Centre Party)	91	64
DVP (People's Party)	19	65
DNVP (National People's Party)	44	71
KPD (Communist Party)	0	4

These results show that the left-wing parties which opposed the republic (especially the Independent Socialists) and the right-wing parties which also opposed it made considerable gains. The three parties which supported the republic (SPD, DDP and Zentrum) lost heavily. Their share of the vote was reduced from 76 per cent to 44 per cent. Thus fewer than half the voters chose a party which supported the republic.

There was now so much hatred between the SPD and the Independent Socialists, that for the government to have a majority, it had to include right-wing parties which wanted to restore the monarchy. This was a pattern which was to persist, and it did not augur well for the future of the republic or for the future of democracy in Germany. The republic was simply not able to win enough loyalty among its own citizens, and it was particularly significant for the future that there was no party backing the republic which had a large following among the powerful Protestant middle class.

One reason why the republican parties did so badly in 1920 and thereafter was that they were blamed for accepting the peace settlement arranged at Versailles by the victorious Allies.

The legacy of the peace settlement

After much bargaining among themselves, the Allies announced to Germany on 1 May 1919 the peace terms that she would have to accept. Almost all sections of German public opinion were outraged. Germany had not been allowed to attend the peace conference at Versailles and practically no notice had been taken of her written comments. The terms imposed were much worse than most Germans had expected. As one recent historian, A. J. Nicholls, has put it:

> 'The German public was in no way prepared for a harsh peace. The Germans had always been told that the Reich was waging a defensive war, and did not therefore regard themselves as responsible for the disaster which had befallen Europe. In any case, the Imperial government and the Emperor were gone, and so the man in the street felt free from all liability for Imperial policies.'
>
> (*Weimar and the Rise of Hitler*)

The German government also expressed its outrage and the prime minister, Scheidemann, resigned. However, it felt that it had no option but to accept, however unwillingly. The Allies threatened to invade Germany if the terms were rejected. They might occupy the industrial areas of western Germany, grant independence to some of the southern states, and watch Germany disintegrate. The government felt that its first duty was to preserve the independence and the unity of the country. However, the republican government was always blamed for having accepted what most Germans regarded as a humiliating and unjust peace.

The terms were contained in a long and complicated document (amounting to 440 clauses). However, the ones which caused most ill-feeling in Germany at the time and had the most serious consequences can be divided into two groups:

War guilt and reparations

The notorious 'war guilt clause' (No. 231) stated that Germany and her allies were responsible for all the damage caused to the Allied governments and their citizens. Germany was to pay for this in different ways. The coal mines of the Saar were to be run by the French for at least fifteen years. Germany was to supply free coal for France, Belgium and Italy. All German merchant ships of over 1600 tonnes (90 per cent of her fleet) were to be surrendered to the Allies. Most important, Germany was to pay indefinitely 'reparations' for damage done to Allied civilians. The amount was to be fixed by a Reparations Commission, which decided that Germany must eventually pay the enormous sum of £6600 million. In addition to arguing that Germany should pay for damage done, the Allies pointed out that Germany's industrial areas had not been devastated as those of France and Belgium had been. It would be unfair, they claimed, if German industry ended the war in a stronger position than that of the victors.

It is generally agreed now that the reparations plan was not very carefully worked out. Germans were bound to resent being controlled by the Reparations Commission and to feel that they were being made to work for their former enemies. There was bound to be an argument with the Allies every time Germany failed to make the full payment. With the benefit of hindsight, reparations were a recipe for trouble.

There was much argument at the time and there has been a great deal of debate among historians ever since about what exactly were the consequences of reparations. Germany paid the first instalment of reparations (£50 million) in 1921, but by 1922 was falling behind. It has been calculated that reparations cost Germany per year only about 2 per cent of her national output. This suggests that the annual payments were not too harsh and that the Allies were right in claiming that Germany simply did not want to pay. On the other hand, the German government also had to face the enormous burden of paying the interest on the loans raised by the imperial government to finance the war. It had been assumed that this cost would in due course be met by Germany's defeated enemies. Now Germany had to pay it in addition to the reparations. Perhaps all of it could have been paid with a struggle, but only by cutting pensions, welfare benefits and so on, and by increasing taxes in a way which would have been very difficult for a weak democratic government.

In January 1923 French and Belgian troops occupied the rich industrial area of the Ruhr with the intention of taking their reparations' payments in coal, steel and manufactured goods. The German government asked the inhabitants of the Ruhr to offer 'passive resistance', which meant that they did not go to work. The German economy suddenly lost a very important source of wealth and, as a result, international confidence in the value of the mark collapsed. In January 1922 one American dollar bought eighty marks. A year later, after the occupation of the Ruhr, a dollar was worth 18,000 marks. We are now used to the process of inflation, by which there is a gradual drop in the value of goods our money will buy. What Germany suffered in 1923 is called 'hyperinflation' because it happened so fast. By November a dollar was worth the amazing figure of 4,420 billion marks. Printing presses struggled to keep up with the demand for new bank notes. Soon they were producing huge numbers of 1 billion mark notes, like the one which can be seen in Figure 6.4.

Fig 6.4   A one billion mark note in 1923.

Old notes soon became quite useless. Figure 6.5 shows children in November 1923 building castles with bundles of worthless paper money.

Fig 6.5 Hyperinflation in 1923 – children building castles with bundles of worthless paper money.

Workers who were lucky enough still to have a job would rush to the shops the moment they were paid in order to buy food before the prices went up, as they often did several times a day. Although their wages were raised they never seemed to keep up with prices. Business was so disrupted by inflation that many people lost their jobs and had to scrape a living in any way they could. Figure 6.6 shows people who became known as 'gleaners'. They had gone from Berlin into the country in October 1923 to scrounge potatoes from the fields. The situation was so desperate that the police were not stopping them, but only supervising them to make sure that there was no disorder.

There has been much argument among historians as to how serious were the consequences of hyperinflation for Germany. There is no doubt that many working people suffered a great deal of hardship as the value of their wages dropped or when they lost their jobs. However, for many of them the problems were short-term. In September a new government called off passive resistance in the Ruhr, and promised to start paying reparations again. As a

Fig 6.6 Potato gleaners: poor Berliners in search of food in 1923.

result, it was possible to put the mark on a new firm footing in mid-November. The economy now began to recover and people gradually got back to work.

Longer-lasting consequences tended to be suffered by middle class people, many of whom saw the value of their savings completely disappear. Some historians have also pointed out that people like businessmen, who had borrowed large sums to buy a factory or machinery or stock for their shops, found that the value of what they had to repay dropped sharply, so they gained in that way. But on balance many middle class people lost badly.

We have seen that the causes of hyperinflation were varied and complex. The Germans did not see it that way. They blamed reparations and the republic which had accepted them and had presided over the chaos of 1923. Many middle class Germans never forgave the republic for the blow they believed it had dealt to them. One of the architects of the Weimar constitution, Hugo Preuss, blamed the Allies, and in 1923 he commented on how the republic had been weakened:

'If the Empire was born out of the brilliance of victory, the German Republic was born out of its terrible defeat. This difference in origin cast from the first a dark shadow on the new political order, as far as national feeling was concerned; but at first most still felt that the new order was necessary for the rebirth of Germany . . . The criminal madness of the imposed Versailles settlement was a shameless blow in the face to such hopes. The Reich constitution of Weimar was born with this curse upon it.

The sight of the impotent misery of the republic made many people forget that Germany was driven into this misery under the old system. And if some fled from the hopeless present into the shadow of the past, others took refuge in heady enthusiasm for mad day-dreams which promised to build a new world on the ruins of all established order. The victorious powers, and France especially, justify their policy of endlessly beating down Germany with the argument that the weakness of the republic and the strength of its enemies means that it may not last. It is precisely this policy which has destroyed the belief that Germany could recover under the republic's constitution.'

The runaway inflation of 1923 had many consequences for Germany. One of the first was a rising in Bavaria in November by a right-wing group which objected to reparations payments being restarted. The rising failed and its leader was imprisoned. However, the world was to hear much more of him later (as we will too in the next two chapters). His name was Adolf Hitler.

Disarmament and land lost

Most Germans also resented the clauses of the Treaty of Versailles which dealt with the disarmament of Germany and the redrawing of the frontiers of Europe. They thought that they were being deliberately humiliated and treated unfairly, and that this treatment of a country which had not been conquered and whose armed forces had not collapsed was unjust.

There is no doubt that the Allies set out to disarm Germany and to prevent her from waging future wars. The German army, which even in 1919 amounted to 300,000 men, was to be greatly reduced in size:

'ARTICLE 160. After March 31st 1920 the total number of effectives in the Army of the state constituting Germany must not exceed one hundred thousand men, including officers and establishments of depots. The Army shall be devoted exclusively to the maintenance of order within the territory and to the control of the frontiers.

The total effective strength of officers must not exceed four thousand.'

The German navy was reduced to a very small size and was not allowed to have any submarines. Germany was to be allowed no military air force. To protect France from the danger of German attack there were to be no German forces to the west of the Rhine or within fifty kilometres of the east bank of that river.

There were two other provisions which were very humiliating for a proud country: there was to be an Allied occupation of German territory to the west of the Rhine for fifteen years, and an Allied Commission of Control in Germany to check that her forces were being kept to the limits set.

If Germans regarded the disarmament clauses as humiliating and vindictive, they thought that the rearrangement of frontiers was an obvious breach of the Allies' own principles. In 1918 and in early 1919 much prominence had been given to the 'Fourteen Points' which the American President, Woodrow Wilson, had hoped would be the basis of the settlement. He believed that an important cause of the war had been the rule by one nation over another, and he called for frontiers to be 'effected along clearly recognisable lines of nationality'. The Versailles peace-makers did try to arrange each nation within its own state, and new national states were set up throughout eastern Europe in the ruins of the Russian and Austro–Hungarian empires – states like Poland, Czechoslovakia and Yugoslavia. Figure 6.7 shows how the frontiers of Europe were rearranged.

Fig 6.7   Germany and the surrounding states after the 1919 peace settlement.

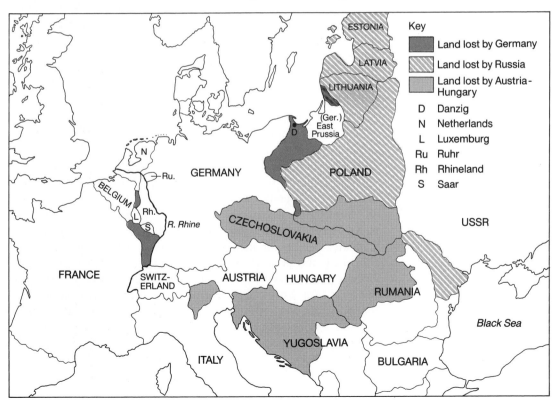

The Germans expected to lose territory in the west. Most did not resent losing Eupen and Malmedy to Belgium, and Alsace and Lorraine to France. After all, Alsace-Lorraine had been taken by Germany when she defeated France in 1871, and the people were French-speaking. However, they thought that elsewhere the rights of nationalities were only recognised when this operated against Germany. West Prussia was given to Poland so that there would be a 'Polish Corridor' giving Poland access to the Baltic Sea at Danzig. This meant that East Prussia was now completely detached from the rest of Germany. Although Danzig was German-speaking, it was to become a 'free port' under the control of the League of Nations, the international organisation set up by the Allies to keep the peace. And although they contained many Germans, Northern Schleswig was allowed to go to Denmark, Upper Silesia to Poland, and Memel to Lithuania. On the other hand, the German Austrians made it clear that they wanted to join Germany now that they had lost their links with Hungary and the other parts of the old Habsburg Empire. They were not allowed to do so, and a separate Austrian state was set up with an entirely German-speaking population. In theory, Germany's colonies were to be ruled for the benefit of their peoples under a 'mandate' or commission of the League of Nations. In practice this meant they went to Germany's colonial rivals (the victorious Allies) as these got the mandates.

To add insult to injury, Germany was not to be allowed to join the League of Nations until she had proved that she was a peace-loving state. Germans had asked the Allies when the war had ended not to treat them as international outcasts. They felt now that this was exactly what had happened, and that they had been treated very unfairly by the peace-makers at Versailles.

Perhaps the Allies would have been wise to allow Germany to attend the peace conference (as France had done in Vienna in 1815), and to admit her at once to the League of Nations. On the other hand, they had a very difficult task. They had to find a compromise between the idealistic proposals of President Wilson and the demands of the French, who wished to punish Germany much more severely than was actually done.

Although the Germans claimed that Wilson's Fourteen Points should have been completely followed, they were not part of the armistice agreement made in November 1918. This means that they had not been guaranteed. In any case the nationalities of Europe were mixed together in a way which made it impossible to draw neat frontiers between them. Given that Germany had lost the war, she was not too harshly treated by the territorial clauses. She lost 13 per cent of her territory, but none of this was a very large area of land with a majority of Germans. The parts that she lost to Poland were the old Polish provinces of Prussia. It is true that, if the principle of recognising nationalities had been fully accepted, Austria would have been allowed to unite with Germany. However, this would have made Germany larger than she had been before the war. The Allies could not be expected to agree to this – especially France, who was very concerned that she might have to fight Germany again. This concern was not unreasonable, since public opinion in Germany was so obviously unwilling to accept responsibility for the war and since (even after 1919) Germany was much larger than France. Her population was 50 per cent greater than that of France. Even as it was, Germany's relative position in Europe had improved with the collapse of the Russian and Austrian Empires. This concern lay also behind the disarmament clauses.

What mattered in Germany was the overall effect of the peace treaty. The prominence given to war guilt, reparations, and the dismantling of the armed forces (of which the Germans had been so proud) seemed to add up to humiliation. It made it seem worse that the republican leaders could not defend the terms, but believed nevertheless that Germany must accept them. This was a realistic assessment. Some Germans said it would be better to refuse the terms, leave it to the Allies to invade if they wished, and then saddle them with the responsibility of imposing their terms on Germany as an occupying force. However, there was every prospect that the Allies would have occupied only the industrialised western areas and left the other German states to fall apart. The Weimar government's acceptance of the terms was almost certainly the best decision for Germany's future. But it looked like abject failure and this seriously weakened the republic, particularly with moderate middle class Germans whose loyalty it might have won. As A. J. Nicholls has put it:

> 'The real damage the treaty did to Germany was to disillusion more moderate men who might otherwise have supported their new Republic... The political gains of the revolution actually had been considerable, but to the public mind they remained unimpressive. The Germans had a new constitution; to many of them the old one had seemed good enough. They had more freedom politically, but most of them had thought of themselves as free before. They had responsible government; this 'responsibility' seemed to mean confusion and even bloodshed in home affairs. The one thing that the new order had brought them – peace – had been transformed by a settlement which their newspapers and political leaders all agreed was a form of prolonged slavery for Germany. It was not an encouraging start.'

(*Weimar and the Rise of Hitler*)

The late twenties – a more secure republic?

There is no doubt that the Weimar Republic did not have a promising start. It failed to win enough active support from its people and faced regular armed risings by extremists of the left and of the right. It took the blame for the humiliating peace treaty in 1919 and the runaway inflation in 1923. In the light of our knowledge of what happened, it is easy to suggest that it was bound eventually to collapse and to be replaced by some sort of dictatorship. But for a time it looked as if the republic could overcome its early problems and become more established.

Hyperinflation in 1923 concentrated the minds of politicians who had previously been unwilling to give the republic their support. One of these was Gustav Stresemann, leader of the right-wing People's Party (the old National Liberals). His party represented many of the leading industrialists, who realised that inflation would put their businesses in serious danger if action were not taken. Stresemann therefore agreed to become chancellor in September 1923. Although he had been violently opposed to the Treaty of Versailles and reparations, he called off passive resistance to the French forces in the Ruhr and agreed to restart payments to the Allies. He thus played a large part in stopping inflation and saving the republic. The National People's Party (the old Conservatives) also began to play its part in government. One of its leaders said:

> 'The republic is beginning to stabilise itself and the German people are becoming reconciled to the way things are. Now is the moment when we must not hesitate. If we wish to retain and reinforce the National People's Party as an influential and powerful movement of the right, we must move to share power in the state.'

At this time it was an attraction to the middle class parties that by joining to form a coalition government they could keep the Majority Socialists (SPD) out of office. But earlier they had not been willing to soften their opposition to the republic even to achieve this. They had still not abandoned their old beliefs, and were sometimes described as 'republicans by necessity'. However, there was reason to hope that more and more people would come to accept the republic if it could be seen to be meeting their needs. This it increasingly did.

After 1923 the economy improved – gradually at first, and then more rapidly. Growth in the economy accelerated after 1924 when Stresemann negotiated the Dawes Plan, which provided for the restart of reparations payments. The total amount due remained unchanged, but the annual payments were reduced. In return for paying reparations, Germany was to receive massive loans from American businesses, some of which were ploughed into updating German factories. By 1927 the national output was higher than it had been in 1913 (despite the fact that the country was now smaller). Exports increased by 40 per cent between 1925 and 1929. But unemployment was rising again in the late 1920s, and some historians claim that this shows that the republic's economic policies were not really working – because, they say, too much was being spent on high wages and on benefits to the old and poor. We will have to return to this argument in the next chapter. However, the fact remains that Germany's economic performance compared favourably with the economic performances of Britain and France between 1925 and 1929.

This prosperity was accompanied by great achievements by German writers, artists and architects. Culture always depends on there being people who are able to pay for it, but in addition there seemed to be something special about the artists of Weimar Germany. It was as if they were excited by a complete freedom which Germans had not enjoyed before. This freedom produced a lively but seedy Berlin night-club scene. The plays of Bertold Brecht; the novels of Heinrich and Thomas Mann; the paintings of Max Ernst, Max Beckmann and Paul Klee; the films of actress Marlene Dietrich; and the architecture of Walter Gropius and Ludwig Mies van der Rohe became famous throughout Europe and have remained so ever since. Some of these artists and architects became known as the 'Bauhaus School', from the name of the school of art and architecture which they built. Figure 6.8 shows the Bauhaus; it set the pattern for many buildings put up around the world during the next half century.

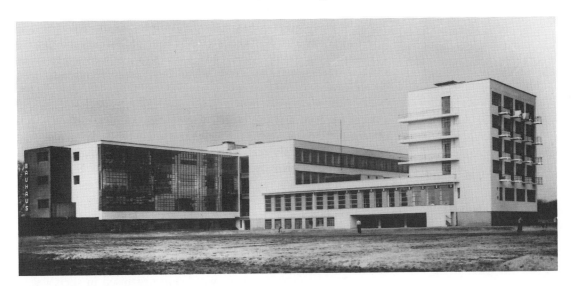

Fig 6.8   The Bauhaus at Dessau.

The Weimar Republic pursued a skilful foreign policy aimed at re-establishing the position of Germany in the world community and at meeting the aspirations of Germans as far as was practicable. Much of the credit for this is also due to Stresemann, who was foreign minister from late 1923 until his death in 1929.

In 1925 Stresemann signed the Locarno Pact, in which Germany accepted her losses in the west and in which Germany and France promised not to attack each other. He much impressed the Allies by the emphasis he put on European co-operation. In a speech he made at Locarno he said to the French foreign minister:

> 'I should like to express to you my deep gratitude for what you said about the necessity of the co-operation of all peoples – and especially of those peoples who have suffered so much in the past. You started from the idea that every one of us belongs in the first instance to his own country, and should be a good Frenchman, German, Englishman, as being a part of his own people, but that everyone also is a citizen of Europe... We have a right to speak of a European idea; this Europe of ours has made such vast sacrifices in the Great War, and yet it is faced with losing, through the effects of the Great War, the position to which it is entitled by tradition and development...
>
> Together with the convulsions of the World War one facet has emerged, namely that we are bound to one another by a single and a common fate. If we go down, we go down together; if we are to reach the heights, we do so not by conflict but by common effort.
>
> For this reason, if we believe at all in the future of our peoples, we ought not to live in disunity and enmity, we must join hands in common labour.'

These promises of co-operation so impressed the Allies that in 1926 Germany was admitted to the League of Nations and given a permanent seat on the Council of the League. She ceased to be an outcast among nations, and her Great Power status was also recognised.

For extreme nationalists in Germany, the price Stresemann had paid at Locarno was too high and they denounced also Germany's consequent admission to the League. However, what he accepted at Locarno was only the settlement in the west, which as we have seen was not Germany's main complaint. He skilfully left open Germany's options in the east. Indeed, as early as 1922, the Weimar government had made the Rapallo Pact, by which Germany and Soviet Russia agreed to co-operate on trade and on some military matters. For example, the German army was allowed to carry out manoeuvres in Russia, far from the prying eyes of the Allies. Even so, the Control Commission was well aware that the German army was being organised in such a way that it could later be expanded very rapidly. For example, it had far more non-commissioned officers than an army of 100,000 needed.

Clearly Weimar Germany did not intend to lie down indefinitely under the arrangements imposed by the hated Versailles Peace Conference. Stresemann certainly aimed to have them changed fundamentally. At the very time that he was negotiating the Locarno Pact, he was making it clear behind the scenes in Germany that he wanted to solve the reparations problem and to win back territory in the east. For example, in September 1925 he wrote to the ex-Crown Prince:

> 'In my opinion there are three great tasks that confront German foreign policy in the more immediate future:
>
> In the first place the solution of the Reparations question in a sense tolerable for Germany, and the assurance of peace, which is essential for the recovery of our strength.
>
> Secondly, the protection of Germans abroad, those 10 to 12 million of our kindred who now live under a foreign yoke in foreign lands.
>
> The third great task is the readjustment of our eastern frontiers; the recovery of Danzig, the Polish Corridor, and a correction of the frontier in Upper Silesia.'

Even in his first speech to the League of Nations Assembly, Stresemann indicated that he hoped the League would assist Germany to change the 1919 settlement – though in much less direct language:

> 'Germany's relations with the League are not confined only to the possibilities of co-operation in general aims and issues. In many respects the League is the heir to the Treaties of 1919. Out of these Treaties there have arisen in the past, I may say frankly, many differences between the League and Germany. I hope that our co-operation within the League will make it easier in the future to discuss these questions.'

By the late 1920s the Weimar Republic was meeting many of the needs of the German people and winning increasing co-operation (if not yet whole-hearted support) from many political parties. In the 1928 Reichstag election the parties which supported the republic received more than half the votes.

In 1930 the Young Plan reduced the total reparations due from £6600 million to £1850 million and ended the much-resented Reparations Commission. Most of this had been negotiated by Stresemann before his death in 1929. The right-wing parties complained that he had sold out by accepting the principle of reparations and that they must be abolished entirely. However, it was a step in that direction.

Is it possible that, given time, the republic could have won the loyalty as well as the co-operation of most of the parties? Is it possible that, given time, it could have reversed some of the most hated terms of the Treaty of Versailles and could thus have blotted out the shame of 1919? Perhaps it could have, but in the event it was not given time. In 1929 it faced a disastrous economic blizzard in which much of what it had achieved was blown away.

ESSAY

Choose one of the following views about the problems of the Weimar Republic, and write an essay to discuss it:

1. 'The Weimar Republic was doomed from the outset because the Social Democrats did not allow the revolution of 1918–19 to clear away the ruling class.'
2. 'The Weimar Republic never had a chance. No German government which dealt with the consequences of defeat in the First World war could have won the affection of its citizens.'
3. 'The major problem of the Weimar Republic was that too few of its citizens wanted to be governed by a republic.'
4. 'In the late 1920s the Weimar Republic was maturing and gaining support. It would have survived if it had not been swept away by the Great Depression.'

The rise of Hitler and the Nazis

On 8 November 1923 a political meeting was being held in a beer hall in Munich. As often happened in Bavaria, the audience sat at tables drinking beer as they listened to the speeches. What was being said was the sort of thing Munich audiences were pretty used to. Munich was a place where many people despised the republic and wanted it to be replaced by something much more right-wing – perhaps some sort of new empire. The only thing that seemed special about this meeting was the speaker. He was Gustav von Kahr, the head of the Bavarian government, and he told his 3000 listeners about the virtues of dictatorship. He spoke on and the beer mugs were filled and refilled.

Suddenly the door was flung open and armed men marched in. They were members of the SA, a private army belonging to the NSDAP, a nationalist party which was growing fast in Bavaria. Among them was the party's leader – Adolf Hitler. Hitler jumped on to a table and fired a shot from his revolver towards the ceiling. He then shouted:

> 'The National Revolution has begun. This building is occupied by 600 heavily armed men. No one may leave the hall. The Bavarian and Reich Governments have been removed and a provisional government formed. The army and police barracks are occupied. The army and the police are marching on the city under the swastika [the NSDAP emblem].'

Most of this was quite untrue. However, Hitler had the advantage of surprise. He also had the advantage that three very important men were now his hostages in the hall. In addition to Kahr there were Lossow, the commander of the army in Bavaria, and General Ludendorff, the wartime leader of the German forces on the western front. The crowd roared in support of Hitler. He demanded that Kahr, Lossow and Ludendorff should join his rising. They would first of all capture Bavaria and then march on Berlin. Ludendorff agreed and the others were with difficulty persuaded to do so (because of the guns being waved at them, they later claimed). Perhaps the alcoholic nature of the occasion had something to do with it. Hitler announced to the by now ecstatic crowd:

> 'I want to fulfil the vow I made to myself five years ago when I was a blind cripple, recovering in a military hospital from a gas

attack at the front – to know neither rest nor peace until the November criminals [the leaders of the revolution in 1918] have been overthrown, until on the ruins of the wretched Germany of today there should arise once more a Germany of power and greatness, of freedom and splendour.'

After this fine speech, things began to go badly wrong. Hitler left the hall to stop trouble outside between regular soldiers and his SA 'storm-troopers'. Kahr and Lossow made good their escape, and soon afterwards issued a statement condemning the rising and making it clear that the army and the police would be used against it.

Ludendorff at least did not change sides and encouraged Hitler to march his men into the centre of Munich the next morning. Surely when it came to the crunch, the police and army would not fire on them. Hitler and Ludendorff shared very similar political views. The storm-troopers were not socialists or strikers.

At first it seemed to have worked. The crowds were friendly to the marchers, and the police could not be seen. However, as they passed through a narrow street near the city centre shots rang out. The police were making a stand. The marcher next to Hitler was shot and dragged Hitler down as he fell. Sixteen marchers were killed and most of the others who could still run (including Hitler) did so. The 'National Revolution', which was to allow Hitler to fulfil his vow and restore Germany to power and greatness, was stopped the morning after it had been launched by a detachment of police. The storm-troopers and their leader ran away. It was an abject and bizarre failure, and (apart from the sixteen deaths) like something from a comic opera.

How was it that Hitler and the Nazi Party, although they appeared in 1923 to be such humiliating failures, were able to get control of the German government ten years later and then rapidly set up a dictatorship?

This question can be answered by dividing it into a number of issues:

1. How did Hitler develop his ideas and why was it important for him to win support for the idea of a 'Führer party' (a party controlled by the leader)?
2. How did Hitler win complete control of his party in 'the time of struggle' up to 1929, when the Nazis did not have a large amount of support?
3. How did Hitler and the Nazis exploit the Great Depression to win mass support between 1929 and 1933? What kind of people voted for them when they won mass support in free elections during the Depression?
4. How was Hitler helped in becoming chancellor in 1933 by the ineffectiveness of his opponents:
a. by more traditional right-wing politicians trying to use Hitler

to replace the Weimar Republic with something of their choosing, but underestimating him and in the event being used by him to clear the way for a Nazi dictatorship?

b. by left-wing parties unable to provide effective opposition because they were weakened by their own quarrels?

5. How did the Nazis get a firm grasp of power in the two months after Hitler became chancellor in January 1933?

These issues raise questions about the *authority* of Hitler and other political leaders and of the Weimar Republic; about the *ideology* of the Nazis and other political parties; and about the sense of *identity* of the German people in a time of unemployment and hardship.

TASK

It is Christmas 1933. Hitler has been German chancellor almost a year and the Nazis are now getting firm control of German life.

You are one of the storm-troopers who marched with Hitler in the Munich Beer Hall Putsch in 1923. You never lost faith in him and soon worked your way up through the ranks to become a high official in the party. This has given you many opportunities to see Hitler at close quarters. You know a lot about how the Nazis have struggled to win power and how they have overcome their enemies.

Now that the struggle has been won and that the Nazis rule Germany, you are going to take time in the Christmas holidays to tell some younger members of your family how these events have happened.

Write down what you are going to tell them. Write in the first person. Your account should describe and explain events roughly in the order in which they happened. You may wish to follow the same sequence as the five sections you will read in this chapter (putting in the Munich Beer Hall Putsch in the appropriate place). Try to give your personal opinion of some of the events, and make some reference to the part you played. However, as a good Nazi your main concern is with Hitler's views and achievements.

Hitler and the Nazi message

Adolf Hitler was born in 1889, the son of a customs official in the Austrian border town of Braunau. He did not do particularly well at school and left at sixteen to go to Linz and later to Vienna. He tried without success to become an artist and was refused entry to the capital's Academy of Graphic Arts. For several years he lived in idle poverty on the fringes of Vienna's artistic community. During this time he became interested in right-wing politics and developed a strong belief in the destiny of the German nation and a bitter hatred of the Jews. In 1913 he moved to Munich. In the following year he greeted the outbreak of the First World War with great enthusiasm and volunteered for the Bavarian army. Hitler was a good soldier and fought throughout the war on the western front, winning the Iron Cross. It is ironic that he was only once given promotion, to lance-corporal, because his officers thought he did not have leadership qualities. However, the war seems to have given him a purpose in life which he did not have before. In 1924 he wrote of the war as the most unforgettable and the greatest time of his life. When the war ended, he was lying in a military hospital, having been temporarily blinded in a mustard gas attack. It was in this state that he heard the news of Germany's defeat and of the revolution. These were bitter blows for someone of Hitler's views, for whom the war had meant so much.

When he recovered, Hitler returned to his regiment in Munich. He shared the strong views of his officers that Germany had not really lost the war, but had been 'stabbed in the back' by the politicians who had made the peace and set up the republic.

He then did propaganda work among soldiers returning from hospitals and prisoner of war camps. It was at this time that his skills as a speaker were developed. One of his superiors described him as 'a born public speaker who through his fanaticism and popular style positively compelled his audience to take note and share his views.'

In September 1919 he was ordered to attend and report on the meetings of a tiny new party, the German Workers' Party (DAP), which was thought to be left-wing. In fact it turned out to be right-wing. Hitler joined, and he soon found in politics the purpose in life that he had lost when the war ended. Figure 7.1 shows Hitler addressing an early meeting of the German Workers' Party. It is clear that he made a great impression on the other members.

In 1920 Hitler played a large part in developing new and more popular policies for the party, and in changing its name to the NSDAP (National Socialist German Workers' Party) or Nazi Party. He was more forceful and a much better speaker than the

Fig 7.1   *Hitler addressing an early meeting of the German Workers' Party.*

Fig 7.2   *SA men in an anti–Communist parade.*

other members. In 1921 he became the party leader and set up its own private army, the SA or 'Storm-troopers'. Their main purpose was at first to keep order at party meetings, but they were increasingly used for street demonstrations and parades. Figure 7.2 shows one of these. It is a march against Marxism; and for the Nazis Marxists meant not only the followers of the Russian Bolsheviks, but also all socialists.

The NSDAP was one of many 'Volkish' parties in Germany at that time. They were all right-wing and nationalist, they opposed the republic and the peace settlement, and they believed that it was important to keep pure the race which made up the 'Volk' (folk) or nation. The two things that gave the NSDAP the advantage were firstly Hitler's absolute certainty that his policies would save Germany, and secondly his gifts as a public speaker. Someone who heard him speak in 1922 wrote that:

> 'I was held under a hypnotic spell by the sheer force of his conviction. The intense will of the man, the passion of his sincerity seemed to flow from him into me. It was like a religious conversion.'

Although Hitler's speeches only seem to have had their full impact on people who already had some sympathy for his views, there were plenty of these about in Bavaria in the early 1920s. By the end of 1922 the NSDAP had about 20,000 members. As people lost their jobs and their savings in the hyperinflation of 1923, party membership grew to about 55,000 immediately before the disastrous Munich Beer Hall Putsch in November.

Hitler was caught and arrested soon after the fiasco, and it could easily have been the end of his political career. Not only had he been made to appear very foolish, but also he was now to be tried on a charge of high treason, which carried a possible life sentence. In fact the trial in early 1924 marked the beginning of his recovery. He was fortunate that (as often happened at that time) the judge and jury had strong right-wing views and did not try to hide them. The judge allowed him to make a long political speech to the jury. He won a lot of admiration by accepting full responsibility for what had happened (unlike Ludendorff, who was in the dock with him) and by defending what he had done. He said:

> 'I alone bear the responsibility, but I am not a criminal because of that. If today I stand here as a revolutionary, it is as a revolutionary against the revolution. There is no such thing as High Treason against the traitors of 1918.'

The jury cheered his speech, and he was sentenced to the minimum of five years in prison, which, as the judge pointed out, would in practice mean much less.

In fact he served only nine months in the reasonable comfort of Landsberg Castle. He was allowed to have his own bodyguards and his secretary with him, and to be visited often by his supporters. He used the time to put the finishing touches to the party programme, which had been taking shape in the early 1920s. The programme was explained in the book he wrote in prison – *Mein Kampf* (My struggle).

Hitler's ideology

Hitler never diverted from the views expressed in *Mein Kampf* and they were the basis of his actions for the rest of his life.

Hitler's most fundamental belief was that race was the thing which determined the current of human affairs, and that the German race was being weakened by the Jews. He explained it this way in *Mein Kampf*:

> 'If we review all the causes which contributed to bring about the downfall of the German people, we shall find that the most profound and decisive cause must be attributed to the lack of insight into the racial problem and especially in the failure to recognise the Jewish danger.
>
> It would have been easy enough to endure the defeats suffered on the battlefields in 1918. They were nothing compared to the military victories which our nation had achieved. Our downfall was not the result of these defeats; but we were overthrown by that force which had prepared those defeats by systematically operating for several decades to destroy these political instincts and that moral stamina which alone enables a people to struggle for its existence. By neglecting the problem of preserving the racial foundations of our national life, the old Empire gave up the sole right which entitles a people to live in this planet. Nations that allow their people to be turned into mongrels sin against the Will of God.'

In other words, Germany had been stabbed in the back in 1918 by Jewish politicians (in left-wing parties such as the SPD), and the empire was to blame for not keeping the German race pure.

These opinions were not unique to Hitler and were based on two views which were common in Europe at that time:

Social Darwinism

Charles Darwin's view was that life in the world of nature is a struggle for survival, with the fit surviving and the weak being destroyed. Social Darwinism applied this view to *human* life. It was claimed that relations between people and nations were also like this: there was bound to be a constant struggle between the strong and the weak. The strong nations would survive and prosper; the weak ones would decline and eventually disappear.

Anti-Semitism

Prejudice against the Jews had been common in Europe for centuries. The Jews had originally been forced to leave Palestine and to find new homes in many lands. However, other peoples had also moved around. In all countries there was a mixture of peoples, whose ancestors had come from different places at different times. What was probably different about the Jews was that they tended to hold on to their own religion and customs. In Christian Europe, therefore, they were obviously distinct. By the late nineteenth century anti-Semitism was still strong, but now that people cared less about religion, it was becoming difficult to defend it on these grounds. As we have seen, nationalism was now becoming a powerful force throughout Europe. Therefore, it became common to defend anti-Semitism on the grounds that Jews diluted the nation and had no real loyalty to it.

Such feelings were becoming stronger in Germany before 1914, because many Jews had fled there from 'pogroms' (persecution) in Russia. This prejudice took new forms after Germany's defeat in 1918. Because of their success in business, Jews were sometimes associated with 'big businessmen', such as bankers, who were seen as having made good profits while other Germans were dying in the trenches. It was also argued (sometimes, quite inconsistently, by the same people) that left-wing parties, from the SPD to the followers of the Russian Bolsheviks, were controlled by Jews. These were the parties, it was argued, which had stabbed Germany in the back in 1918 by making peace and setting up the republic, and were still doing their best to destroy what was left of the German way of life.

These arguments were based on prejudice, ignorance and a highly selective use of half-understood facts. However, in a country which had suffered such blows to its pride and prosperity as Germany had done between 1918 and 1923, such ideas became popular. People wanted an explanation for what had gone wrong which would save their pride, and it was not only Hitler and the Nazis who offered these particular explanations. It suited many Germans to see the Jews as scapegoats.

Hitler's programme was more generally accepted than those of the many other anti-Semitic nationalists in Germany. What he was able to offer his public, battered by the storms of ill-fortune, was his complete certainty that he could solve their problems. He could lift their gaze from their immediate troubles and give them a fully worked-out view of the world which (however illogical and repellent it may seem to us) made sense to them. He did this by oratory which almost cast a spell over people who were already sympathetic to his message. The foundation of his view of the world was his all-consuming hatred of the Jews. He saw them as mounting a world conspiracy against other races. This extract from a speech he made in 1922 gives a flavour of the extreme language he used against the Jews:

'The Jews are a people of robbers. He has never founded any civilisation, though he had destroyed civilisations by the hundred. He possesses nothing of his own creation to which he can point ... He has no art of his own; bit by bit he has stolen it all from the other peoples or has watched them at work and then made his copy. He does not even know how merely to preserve the precious things which others have created; as he turns the treasures over in his hand they are transformed into dirt and dung'.

In a notorious and prophetic passage in *Mein Kampf* he asserted that a million Germans killed at the front during the war could have been saved if 'twelve to fifteen thousand of these Hebrew corrupters of the people had been held under poison gas'. The Jews were a particular threat to the 'Aryan race' (Germans) because it was the only really creative race in the world. The German race must thus be 'purified'. He argued in *Mein Kampf* that:

'All great cultures of the past perished only because the originally created race died out from blood poisoning ... Blood mixture and the resultant drop in the racial level is the sole cause of the dying out of old cultures.'

However, the Jewish threat came not only from such people as bankers and socialist politicians within Germany. By 1922 Hitler had also come to the conclusion that the Bolshevik revolution in Russia was a Jewish conspiracy. The twin threats to the traditional German way of life were the Jews and the Bolsheviks (or, as we would call them, communists). Both could be defeated by a life-or-death struggle in eastern Europe, in which Germany would destroy the Russian revolutionaries and at the same time obtain 'Lebensraum' (living space) for her people to settle in and to which to sell her products. Thus the defeat of the 'Jewish and Bolshevik plots' would also guarantee German prosperity.

In the past some historians thought that Hitler was merely an opportunist who made the most of chances as they appeared. However, most now believe that he had always aimed to invade Russia and eventually did so. For example, Ian Kershaw has written that:

'By the mid-1920s, then, Hitler had developed a rounded philosophy which offered him a complete view of the world, its ills and how to overcome them. Its substance never changed down to his death ... When the show-down with 'Jewish Bolshevism' eventually became reality with the invasion of the Soviet Union in 1941, it was for Hitler – and not for him alone – the culmination of this "crusading" idea.'

(*Hitler*)

It is easy to see why the National Socialist German Workers' Party (NSDAP) called itself a 'national' party. It carried to new and extreme lengths the nationalism which had built up in the nineteenth and early twentieth centuries in Germany (and in other countries). It is more difficult to work out why it also claimed to be a 'socialist' party. Hitler's hatred of the Bolsheviks would lead us to expect, correctly, that he did not want to destroy private property or to redistribute it to the workers. He regarded farmers, small shopkeepers and skilled craftsmen as pillars of the community. It was big business that he distrusted, and he spoke of such moves as the state taking over chains of department stores and leasing them to small shopkeepers. It is true that the Nazis did impose some controls over big business, but this side of the Nazi programme was not developed far. Despite their claim to be socialist, the Nazis took care never to threaten German businessmen seriously.

The Nazis did not specifically say that they wished to destroy parliamentary democracy. On the other hand, they often alleged that democratic politicians were corrupt. Their increasing emphasis on the obedience due by all to the 'Führer' (leader) made it clear enough what would happen to democracy if the Nazis won control. During his nine months in Landsberg Castle in 1924, Hitler came to the conclusion that he was the great leader who would rescue Germany. The purpose of *Mein Kampf* was to make this known to the German people. Thereafter, Hitler did everything he could to ensure that his orders were accepted without question – first in the Nazi Party and later in the whole of Germany.

Hitler wins control of the Nazi Party

The collapse of the Munich Beer Hall Putsch in 1923 might have marked the end of Hitler's political career. In fact he returned from his nine months' imprisonment in a stronger position within the party. This was partly because he had given such an impressive and courageous performance at his trial. It was also partly because he had used his time at Landsberg to finalise his programme and to write *Mein Kampf*: this enabled him to give the party faithful a clearer and more compelling vision of where they were going than any of its other leaders could. In addition it was partly because the other leaders had been quarrelling for most of the nine months that he had been away, and only his personality could keep them together.

Hitler had a very firm personal hold on the other leading Nazis. He never became over familiar, but he would dominate the conversation with his strong views on many subjects. He read widely and had a very good memory for detail. This enabled him to overwhelm in argument anyone who dared to disagree with him. However, fear of his tongue alone would not have bound them to him in the 1920s, when he brought them few material benefits. They admired enormously his clear view of the world and of how he would put it to rights. For example, Rudolf Hess referred to 'the power of personality, radiating something that puts those around him under its spell and spreads in ever-widening circles'. It was when he was Hitler's secretary at Landsberg that Hess fully understood the 'mighty significance' of Hitler's personality. When Joseph Goebbels read *Mein Kampf*, he asked 'Who is this man? Half working man, half God! Truly Christ, or only St John?' Even when he was in prison after Hitler's death, Alfred Rosenberg spoke of Hitler's great belief in his people and in his mission, his creative drive, and his iron will. Despite many rivalries and feuds among themselves, the other Nazi leaders were united in their respect for Hitler.

After 1924 Hitler gradually developed the admiration of the other Nazi leaders into something more formal – an unquestioning obedience to the word of the Führer. In 1926 Hitler overcame demands from a group of north German Nazis under Gregor Strasser that the party programme should be revised. Among other things they wanted it to be more socialist. However, Hitler's main argument was that by putting forward such demands, they were rejecting his authority. Hitler got his way at a party congress and no one in the party ever again publicly argued with him over policy. It was now accepted that he made all the important decisions on policy and on how the party should be run. It was at this time that party members began to greet each other by saying 'Heil Hitler!' (Hail Hitler).

Between 1924 and 1929 circumstances did not allow the Nazi Party to do well in elections. Large numbers of Germans were not likely to opt for the extreme solutions proposed by the Nazis in years when most felt reasonably prosperous. The Nazis called this the 'time of struggle'. However, in these years, Hitler made clear the mission that he believed he had to save Germany, and he established among his own supporters that this could only be achieved by unquestioning loyalty to the Führer. This enabled the Nazis to build up an invincible position on the extreme nationalist right-wing of German politics. In 1929 there were over 100,000 paid-up members.

Hitler's approach also meant that when economic disaster in 1929 sent many Germans looking for a strong new leader, he had all the credentials.

Hitler wins mass support

Despite Hitler's growing authority within the Nazi Party and among Germans who shared his views, these people were still a small minority in 1928. The Nazis won only 2.6 per cent of the vote and twelve seats in the Reichstag election of that year.

Their efforts to widen their appeal were helped in July 1929 by an invitation to join a group of right-wing parties to campaign against the Young Plan (see page 141). The group was brought together by Alfred Hugenberg, who owned many newspapers and was the leader of the DNVP (National People's Party). Like many nationalists he objected to Germany making any agreement which accepted that reparations would continue (even at a lower level). He thought that he could use Hitler as a 'drummer' to win support for his campaign and he gave him much more coverage in his newspapers than Hitler had ever had before. The result was that the Nazis gained a new respectability among many Germans. Hugenberg was by no means the last aristocratic politician who thought that he could use Hitler for his own ends, but in the event was used by him. We will return to this theme on page 163.

The Great Depression

Nevertheless, Hitler would almost certainly have remained on the extremist fringe of politics had it not been for the Great Depression, which began in 1929, and the hardship it brought. It was this which enabled him to build up mass support. We have seen that by the summer of 1929 there were already signs that the years of prosperity were slipping away. Most notably there were already around two million unemployed. Another bad sign was that less money was being invested by businessmen in new factories and equipment. However, the event which plunged the world into economic disaster was 'The Great Crash' on Wall Street, the New York Stock Exchange.

On 'Black Friday' in October 1929 the value of shares dropped disastrously. Financiers who had lost everything threw themselves off the top of New York skyscrapers. This was the melodramatic opening of a depression which in the following years was to cause great distress all over the world. People who owned shares were suddenly very much poorer. Those who had put their savings in bank accounts saw them disappear as the banks collapsed. Many people stopped buying anything except essentials. Jobs were lost in factories around the world, in the mines and steelworks which supplied them, on the ships which carried the goods and in the shipyards which would otherwise have been building new ships. People could not afford to eat so much and farm prices dropped. Farmers then could not afford to spend, and so it went on.

It was a strange coincidence that Stresemann, who in a sense represented the good years of the Weimar Republic, died in the same month as the Wall Street Crash.

There is no doubt that Germany suffered particularly badly from the Depression. Americans now demanded repayment of the large loans made under the Dawes Plan (see page 138). Businesses which had invested American money in new equipment were unable to repay it immediately. As a result they went bankrupt, adding further to the unemployment which was soaring in all countries. By December 1930 three million Germans were unemployed, by July 1931 5.5 million and by January 1932 over six million. Because so many people were spending less, the taxes paid to the government dropped sharply. To try to make ends meet, it reduced the salaries of government employees by a quarter and so they had less to spend. Perhaps the unkindest cut of all was that, because there were so many unemployed and because it was so short of money, the government cut the rate of unemployment benefit by over a half. The Depression caused a great deal of suffering for very many people in Germany – worse than what was experienced in Britain and France.

At first one of the most shocking features was the speed with which people could be thrown into poverty. Figure 7.3 shows some very well dressed people in a soup kitchen queue in 1930.

Fig 7.3   A queue at a soup kitchen in 1930.

An American journalist described a restaurant in a working class area of Berlin which was full of people, but where nobody could afford to order even the poor food which was available:

'An iron screen guarded the buffet and behind the bars lay a fly-speckled platter of fried horse-meat and a pair of horse-meat sausages. The guests were hungry. They sat at their tables and gazed through the bars at the horse-meat. It was dinner time, but they ordered nothing. Their hunger was nothing to do with dinner time. Of forty guests in the restaurant only two had anything on their table. Between one old man and a slovenly woman stood a beaker of malt beer. First he took a sip, put the beaker down and stared at the horse-meat. They were the liveliest guests in the room until we came in.'

Some of the unemployed could not afford a bed to sleep in or even a space on someone's floor. Figure 7.4 shows them sleeping over a rope in what was called a 'flop house'.

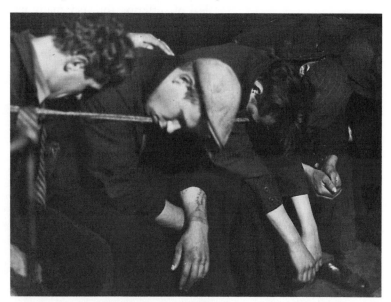

Fig 7.4   Unemployed workers sleep over a rope in a Hamburg 'flop house'.

There was nothing inevitable about the rise to power of the Nazis. There were many reasons and, as we shall see, many people can be held responsible. However, the essential factor without which they would never have ruled Germany was the misery caused by the Depression. It was now that, for the first time, they won mass support. In the Reichstag election of September 1930 their seats shot up from twelve to 107. With over 18 per cent of the vote they were now the second largest party (after the SPD). In July 1932 the Nazis won the largest vote a party ever received in a free election in the Weimar Republic: 37 per cent of the votes and 230 seats.

This does not, however, mean that most of the extra Nazi votes were from the unemployed (although Hitler claimed that he was their last hope). Many Germans who were suffering from the Depression were more likely than unemployed workers to vote for an extreme right-wing party. For example, there were farmers and small businessmen whose businesses were in ruins or just in trouble. There were teachers and civil servants whose salaries had been cut. There was also the great army of people who were simply afraid of losing their jobs. It has been shown that almost everyone in Germany during the Depression thought that they might become unemployed. In Britain, by contrast, only around half the workforce feared for their jobs and white-collar workers were reasonably safe.

Who voted for the Nazis?

To understand how the Nazis built up mass support during the Depression, we must look at the sort of people who voted for them at the peak of their electoral success in July 1932. It used to be claimed that the supporters of the Nazi Party were lower middle class people, such as small shopkeepers, self-employed craftsmen, clerks and junior civil servants. But recent research has shown that their support was much wider and much more complex than that. Substantial numbers of manual workers did vote for Hitler, but most did not. It was in working class districts of large cities that the Nazis did worst. Manual workers might vote for left-wing parties like the SPD and the communists (which between them won almost as many votes as the Nazis in July 1932 and slightly increased their total number of votes). Many Catholic workers voted for the Catholic Zentrum Party. The best Nazi performance in the big cities was in the richest suburbs. On the whole, neither large cities nor Catholic areas returned the largest Nazi vote: that is where the votes of Zentrum, the SPD and the communists held up reasonably well. Where the Nazis did best was in small towns and in the countryside, especially in the Protestant north. In many such areas the Nazis seemed to be able to offer something to most people, and in some places over 80 per cent voted Nazi.

Hitler and the Nazis used two very important methods to win the support of such a wide range of people:

Interest groups

The Nazis set up groups representing the interests of many different sections of the population – farmers, doctors, lawyers, students, school and university teachers, civil servants, small businessmen, young people, women and even manual workers. These groups set out to show that the Nazis understood their particular worries (and in Depression Germany every group had serious worries) and would try to help them. The interests of some of these people were opposed to those of others. The Nazis, therefore, gave contradictory promises. Nevertheless, people were won over by the Nazis' apparent concern for 'bread and butter issues' as well as by Hitler's more ambitious claims.

Propaganda

There is no doubt that Hitler's main appeal during the misery of the Depression was his claim that only he could save Germany and he used great skill to put across this message. He had to build up among potential supporters a belief in 'The Führer's Mission'.

Hitler could, as always, be relied on to whip into a frenzy of enthusiasm those sufficiently interested to come to his meetings, so up-to-date methods were used to try to get him in front of as many people as possible. When he campaigned to be elected president in March 1932 an aeroplane was chartered to fly him from meeting to meeting. The skilful slogan 'The Führer Over Germany' was coined by the Nazis' propaganda chief, Dr Joseph Goebbels.

Since most voters could never see Hitler personally in those days before television, Goebbels's role was vital in spreading the message. His brilliant propaganda techniques played a large part in exploiting the Depression to win mass support for the Führer and his party. He had studied American advertising and publicity techniques, and he used them to the full. He was a master of political posters, always with a neat slogan. One of the most famous showed Hitler under the message 'I have millions behind me.'

Fig 7.5 and Fig 7.6 Nazi banners being paraded in the 1930 Reichstag election campaign.

Nazi marches and rallies were organised across the country,
often in small towns which rarely saw a political meeting. These
rallies offered much excitement with bands, marching men and
banners. Figures 7.5 and 7.6 show a rally and a march organised
by the Nazis during the 1930 election campaign. They give an
idea of the colour and excitement of these events.

By 1932 it was even easier for the Nazis to put on a good show.
They now had 800,000 members and almost half a million storm-
troopers. The message was expressed in simple black and white
statements. The flavour is given by an extract from one of
Goebbels's pamphlets:

'WHY ARE WE NATIONALISTS?

We are NATIONALISTS because we see in the NATION the only
possibility for the protection and furtherance of our
existence...

It was the sin of MARXISM to degrade SOCIALISM to a system
of MONEY and STOMACH.

We are SOCIALISTS because for us THE SOCIAL QUESTION IS A
MATTER OF NECESSITY AND JUSTICE, and even beyond that A
MATTER FOR THE VERY EXISTENCE OF OUR PEOPLE.

SOCIALISM IS POSSIBLE ONLY IN A STATE WHICH IS FREE INSIDE
AND OUTSIDE.

DOWN WITH MIDDLE CLASS SENTIMENTALITY! UP WITH REAL
NATIONALISM!

DOWN WITH MARXISM! UP WITH TRUE SOCIALISM!

UP WITH THE STAMP OF THE FIRST GERMAN NATIONAL SOCIALIST
STATE!

AT THE FRONT THE NATIONAL SOCIALIST GERMAN WORKERS'
PARTY!'

The message was designed to play on the anger of the listeners
at what they were suffering and their fear that worse might be to
come, and to assure them that the Führer's leadership would solve
the problems of the nation. As Ian Kershaw has put it:

'Hitler inspired the millions attracted to him by the conviction
that he and he alone, backed by his Party, could end the current
misery and lead Germany to new greatness. The vision of the
future held the promise of great benefits for all – as long as they
were racially fit – while those enemies of the people who had
hitherto held them in thrall would be not only banished, but
completely extirpated.'

(*Hitler*)

Marxists were the 'enemies of the people' who were usually
highlighted. They, it was said, were planning to exploit the
business crisis and the misery of the unemployed to set up a
Bolshevik dictatorship in Germany. A vote for Hitler was claimed
to be the best protection against this threat, the fear of which
united the various groups likely to favour the Nazis. The SA was
used by the Nazis to stir up street fighting with communists and
other left-wingers. This kept the 'Bolshevik threat' in the minds
of Hitler's potential supporters and gave them the impression that
law and order were breaking down and that only the Nazis could
restore them. In reality, the Nazis (and the communists) were
creating disorder for their own ends. Although Nazi speakers
were always liable to bring it up, not so much emphasis was put
on the 'Jewish question' during elections.

Hitler's victory over the politicians

In July 1932 Hitler had the support of 37 per cent of the German
voters. He had won the backing of more people than any other
party in the history of the Weimar Republic. But this was not
enough to win him control of the state. When he asked President
Hindenburg to appoint him chancellor, he received a point-blank
refusal. The constitution of the Weimar Republic did not oblige
the president to make the leader of the largest party chancellor.
After so much effort and so much success for the Nazi Party, this
was a devastating anti-climax. There were even whispers in its
ranks that the Führer had been wrong to insist that he would enter

a government only as chancellor. The party began to lose members and voters. When another Reichstag election was called in November 1932, the Nazis received two million fewer votes and 34 fewer seats. However, with 33 per cent of the vote they were still the largest party, and Hitler renewed his demand to be made chancellor. This time Hindenburg did not even meet him, but had his secretary send this letter:

> 'The President thanks you, my dear Herr Hitler, for your willingness to take on the leadership of a presidential cabinet. But he believes he could not justify it to the German people if he were to give powers to the leader of a party which has usually opposed the President personally and the economic and political measures he has considered necessary. In these circumstances the President must fear that a cabinet led by you would develop into a dictatorship. The President in view of his oath [to the constitution] and his conscience could not take the responsibility for this.'

At the end of 1932 it seemed to some that Hitler had shot his bolt and failed. The Nazi Party was short of money and demoralised. However, by a month later he was chancellor of Germany, and by three months later he had set up a powerful dictatorship. What had changed in that time was that he had managed to outmanoeuvre the politicians of the Weimar Republic.

The last government of the Weimar Republic which was based firmly on a Reichstag majority resigned in March 1930. It fell because the Social Democrats would not accept proposed cuts in unemployment benefit. President Hindenburg appointed as the new chancellor Dr Heinrich Bruning. Although he was a member of the Centre Party, he really wanted to replace the Weimar Republic by a more authoritarian state, perhaps something like the old empire in Bismarck's heyday. As we have seen, such views were not uncommon. What was more ominous for German democracy was that the president and the army commanders wanted Bruning to move the republic in that direction. They had never been enthusiastic about parliamentary democracy. The squabbling over unemployment benefit convinced them that a democratic government could not solve the problems of the Depression – especially as the parties were allocated seats in the Reichstag according to the percentage of the vote they had won (proportional representation) and so it was impossible for one party to get a majority. Bruning was unable to get enough support in the Reichstag and called an election in September 1930 (two years earlier than was necessary). He hoped his allies would do well and would give him a Reichstag majority, but in the event it was the Nazis and communists who made gains. It was an ominous sign for the future of German democracy that President Hindenburg allowed Bruning to carry on as chancellor for almost another two years and to rule under Section 48 of the Weimar Constitution:

> 'Where public security and order are seriously disturbed or endangered within the Federation, the President of the Federation may take the measures necessary for their restoration, intervening in case of need with the help of armed forces. For this purpose he is permitted, for the time being, to put aside either wholly or partially some of the fundamental laws . . .
>
> The President of the Federation must, without delay, inform the Reichstag of any measures taken in accordance with this article. Such measures shall be withdrawn upon the command of the Reichstag.'

Some historians have argued that this was not a fatal blow to democracy in Germany. The same article had been used in 1923 to enable Stresemann to end hyperinflation. Public order, they say, was threatened as much by the Depression in 1930 as it had been by inflation. In any case, the Reichstag still had the power to reject any measure taken by the government.

There were, however, important differences between 1923 and the early 1930s. In 1923 Section 48 was used for only a few months by men who wanted to return to full parliamentary democracy as soon as possible. In the early thirties it was used for three years by men who were meantime looking for a more authoritarian form of government. The effect of governing under Section 48 for such a long period was to put effective power into the hands of the president and the group of right-wing politicians and army officers which surrounded him. None of these men believed that the constitution of the republic was suited to the task of getting Germany out of the Depression.

Bruning certainly had a clear view of how the government should deal with the Depression, and he carried it out with determination. As so much less business was being done, the amount of taxes paid to the government dropped sharply. Bruning believed that the government must 'balance its books' by raising tax rates and cutting spending (in particular by cutting unemployment benefit and the salaries of civil servants). This, of course, meant that people had even less to spend and made the Depression even worse. Bruning argued that, however painful this was, it was necessary. If the government did not balance its books, people would lose confidence in the German mark and inflation would be set off again, as in 1923. Thus the temporary pain was needed to ensure that Germany came out of the Depression in good shape. Furthermore, the obvious poverty of Germany during the Depression would make it easier to demand an end to the hated reparations payments, which all Germans wanted to see.

Bruning's policy undoubtedly brought great hardship to many Germans and he became known as 'The Hunger Chancellor'.

Historians used to argue that Bruning's policy was wrong and that the desperation it unnecessarily caused played a large part in allowing Hitler to win power. Nowadays a more common view is that Bruning could not have followed a policy which was fundamentally different. Economists no longer believe, as they did for forty years after the 1930s, that to get out of a depression a government should spend rather than cut back. Furthermore, it was natural that after the horrors of 1923 Germans should have a great fear of inflation and should be determined to avoid it at all costs.

Perhaps, some historians say today, Bruning did not need to be quite so harsh. Perhaps he could have afforded to order the building of more hospitals, schools and houses, which would have shown that some people were getting back to work. He certainly did not need to put up taxes on food imports in order to allow East Elbian landowners to continue selling their produce at high prices. Lower food prices would have done something to ease the plight of the unemployed. Perhaps if Bruning had made his policy slightly less harsh, the Nazis could have been held at bay for long enough to allow them to fall apart. Historians who argue this, point out that the Nazis were losing support at the end of 1932. If only the republic could have held on a little longer!

However, Bruning did not want to preserve the Weimar Republic. He wanted to strengthen the power of the central government at the expense of the Reichstag and of the state governments (in Prussia, Bavaria, and so on). Eventually he hoped that the monarchy could be restored. He hoped that the popular support he expected to win by ending reparations would enable him to do these things. He thought that he could use Hitler and the Nazis to achieve his own ends. Other politicians tried this, before and after 1930. Invariably it was Hitler who used them.

In October 1930 Bruning met Hitler. He told him that he expected that the economic crisis would last for several years and that he was relying on Hitler's campaign against the Treaty of Versailles to help persuade the Allies to end reparations. Hitler did nothing to assist Bruning, but continued to exploit the problems of the Depression to attract the support of many groups in Germany.

Among those from whom Hitler hoped to win support were the owners of Germany's heavy industries. Although under the pressure of revolution in 1919 they had reached an agreement with the trade unions, many resented the restrictions the Weimar Republic had put on their freedom of action. In the late 1920s they had complained that when there was a dispute with the unions over wages, they were forced to go to arbitration and that this

forced up wages. Many industrialists longed for a more authoritarian government which would keep the workers in their
place. Many were also unenthusiastic about Stresemann's quest
for international agreements and wanted a more aggressive foreign
policy which would require armaments made by their factories.
This seemed even more desirable as they had lost orders and
profits during the Depression. It was natural, therefore, that
Hitler should try to enlist their support. In January 1932 he made
a speech to the Industry Club in Düsseldorf:

> 'Today the Nazi Movement cannot be destroyed; it is there;
> people must reckon with it whether they like it or not. For here
> they see before them an organisation inspired to the highest
> degree by national sentiment, constructed on the conception of
> an absolute authority in the leadership of all spheres, at every
> stage – the solitary party which amongst its members has
> completely overcome not only the conception of
> internationalism but also the idea of democracy, which in its
> entire organisation acknowledges only the principles of
> Responsibility, Command and Obedience... And when people
> cast in our teeth our intolerance, we proudly acknowledge it –
> yes, we have formed the inexorable decision to destroy
> Marxism in Germany down to its very last root.'

This was exactly what most industrialists wanted to hear, and
this speech certainly won for Hitler the sympathy of some of
them. It was argued by Hitler's opponents that he was a tool of
the owners of industry and that he would not have come to power
without their financial backing. For example, these opponents
turned against him the famous Nazi slogan 'I have millions behind
me' with a poster of their own, in which a factory owner is
shown behind Hitler passing him wads of banknotes. It is now
known that only a few industrialists gave Hitler large sums of
money during his rise to power. Many gave him modest sums,
but they gave much more to other right-wing parties which
might forward their views. Till Hitler became chancellor in 1933,
most of the Nazis' funds were raised by themselves through
collections at their many meetings and rallies. It was only when
the Nazis were in power that they started to receive large sums
from many industrialists. It is not fair, therefore, to suggest that
the support of industrialists played a major part in Hitler's rise to
power. It was mainly politicians who for their own ends eventually
put his hands on the levers of power.

It was one of the weaknesses of government through Section 48
of the Weimar constitution that, since the president was now over
eighty years old, a great deal of influence was put into the hands
of his cronies. One of the most powerful of these was General von
Schleicher, who represented the views of the army leadership. By

the spring of 1932 he and the other generals had lost patience with Bruning. Their concern was not the suffering of so many hungry people. Instead they wanted him to get rid of the Social Democrats still in positions of influence (for example, in the state government of Prussia). They were outraged when in the presidential election of March 1932 most right-wing votes went to Hitler. Hindenburg was only re-elected by the Social Democrats and the Catholic supporters of Zentrum. They considered this a humiliation for the 'war hero' and the army which supported him, and they blamed Bruning. Since Bruning had been put in by the president, he could be put out by him, and Schleicher arranged this in May 1932. The immediate excuse for this was that the Nazi private army, the SA, had been banned because it was causing so much disorder. Schleicher saw this as a surrender to the communists with whom the storm-troopers most frequently brawled.

Schleicher played a large part in choosing an even more right-wing government under Franz von Papen. It was called 'the Cabinet of Barons' because it contained so many landowners. Schleicher and Papen thought they could win the support of the Nazis by ending the ban on the SA and by dismissing in July 1932 the government of Prussia. Prussia was by far the largest of the states of Germany and, because it contained most of the industrial areas, now had a Social Democrat government. The Prussian government stood in the way of Schleicher and Papen in making a more authoritarian state, but it also stood in the way of Hitler's ambitions in the same direction. He was delighted, but he did not give Papen any thanks for this or for ending the ban on the SA. On the contrary, Nazi propaganda attacks on the republic and the SA's brawling on the streets were stepped up. The Nazi band-wagon gathered speed and in the Reichstag elections on 31 July Hitler won more than a third of the total vote.

A pattern had now been established of right-wing politicians believing that they could use the Nazis to bring about the sort of authoritarian Germany they wanted, but actually playing into Hitler's hands. The pattern was continued in late 1932. After calling further elections in November, in the vain hope of getting a Reichstag majority, Papen showed his true colours. He now proposed to the president that the Reichstag should be dissolved and that Germany should be ruled by government decree and by army courts until a new authoritarian constitution could be drawn up. This is how he explained it later in his memoirs:

'There seemed no reason to suppose that the newly-elected Reichstag should not behave in exactly the same way as the previous one. If the government was not to be permitted to function, then it must do without the Reichstag altogether for a short period. Our proposed amendments to the constitution would then be made the subject of a referendum or submitted for approval to a new National Assembly. This procedure, I realised, would involve a breach of the present constitution by the President.

The situation was so serious that I considered that the President might be justified in placing the welfare of the nation above his oath to the constitution . . . I reminded him of the manner in which Bismarck had once found it necessary to recommend to the Prussian monarch that the constitution should be ignored for the sake of the country.'

This was too direct for the army, and in December Schleicher himself became chancellor in place of Papen. However, Papen was soon scheming to return to government, and in January 1933 he managed to put together a right-wing coalition of representatives of the army and of industry, landowners, and (for the first time) the Nazis. Hitler was to be given the post of chancellor that he had demanded after his two 1932 election victories. However, the Nazis were to be given only two other ministries, and Papen was to be given strong powers as vice-chancellor. The Nazis would bring to the new government the mass support and the Reichstag seats which it would otherwise lack.

Papen and the other groups backing the government were sure that they could keep the Nazi chancellor and the two Nazi ministers in order. Perhaps this is why they took the Nazis into government, when the November 1932 elections showed that the Nazis' support was falling. They thought that the Nazi leaders would now have to be more reasonable. They were mistaken – tragically for Germany and for millions of people outside Germany.

All through the night of 30 January 1933 Hitler took the salute from the window of his new office in the chancellery as the storm-troopers paraded past. Within two months he had the powers for a Nazi dictatorship.

Without the Depression Hitler would have been unable to build up mass support. However, without the help of right-wing politicians who thought that they could use him for their own ends, he could not have won power. Ian Kershaw explains it like this:

'The handover of power to Hitler on 30 January 1933 was the worst possible outcome to the irrecoverable crisis of Weimar democracy. It did not have to happen. It was at no stage a foregone conclusion . . . Had powerful groups like the army, landowners and industrialists opposed it, a Hitler Chancellorship would have been inconceivable. Hitler needed them to attain power. But in January 1933 they in turn needed Hitler since he alone could deliver the mass support required to impose an authoritarian solution to Germany's crisis.'

(*Hitler*)

It may seem surprising that the left-wing parties did not do more to prevent the Nazis from winning power. After all, they stood to lose most in a Nazi Germany. The KPD (the German Communist Party) made no attempt to save the republic, but did everything it could to add to the chaos. It was under orders from its masters in Moscow to try to bring down parliamentary democracy in the expectation that this would pave the way for a workers' revolution. Many German communists died because this did not happen.

The behaviour of the SPD (the Social Democrats) is more curious. They continued to argue and to vote for parliamentary democracy, as they had done throughout the history of the Weimar Republic. However, they were unwilling to use the force of their trade union allies. In 1920 the Kapp Putsch was defeated by an immediate general strike across Germany, but in July 1932 no such strike followed Papen's dismissal of the Social Democrat government of Prussia. It has been argued that the two situations were not comparable. It may be that the depth of a depression was a poor time to organise a general strike. Those lucky enough to have jobs may have been too concerned to keep them. On the other hand, the behaviour of the SPD leaders suggests that they were weary and dispirited by the early 1930s. For example, they gave Bruning informal backing with their Reichstag votes throughout his chancellorship. They may indeed have feared something worse, but a more powerful political force would have been less willing to support a chancellor who was obviously no friend of the SPD's democratic ideals or of the people the party represented. It may be that the SPD's leaders had been worn down by the bitter feuding between left-wing parties which went back to the earliest days of the republic and even before that.

The Nazi dictatorship is established

The right-wing politicians who had made Hitler chancellor thought that they could control him, and Papen told one of his friends 'We've hired him.' They were soon disabused of such thoughts.

The Nazis at once spoke of 'the seizure of power'. A campaign was immediately started against members and officials of left-wing parties. They were beaten up and in many cases arrested by the SA and by other Nazis. The prisons were soon full and the first concentration camps were set up. Some of those arrested were killed. One of the leading Nazis, Hermann Göring, was made Prussian Minister of the Interior, and he therefore controlled the police over a large part of Germany. In an order on

17 February 1933 he made very clear what he expected of the Prussian police:

> 'I assume it is unnecessary to point out especially that the police must in all circumstances avoid giving even the appearance of a hostile attitude towards, still less the impression of persecuting, the patriotic associations [the SA and other Nazis]. I expect all police authorities to maintain the best relations with these organisations which comprise the most important constructive forces of the State. Patriotic activities and propaganda are to be supported by every means.
>
> The activities of subversive organisations are on the contrary to be combated with the most drastic methods. Communist terrorist acts and attacks are to be proceeded against with all severity, and weapons must be used ruthlessly when necessary. Police officers who in the execution of this duty use their firearms will be supported by me without regard to the effect of their shots; on the other hand, officers who fail from a false sense of consideration may expect disciplinary measures ... Every official must constantly bear in mind that failure to act is more serious than errors committed in acting. I expect and hope that all officers feel themselves at one with the aim of saving our fatherland from the ruin which threatens it by strengthening and unifying the patriotic forces.'

The police sometimes assisted in the campaign of violence and at other times merely did nothing to stop it. It was in this atmosphere of fear that Hitler called Reichstag elections for 5 March. The Nazis could now use the power of the state to terrorise their opponents in the newspapers, on the streets, and at meetings. For example, on 4 February the president was persuaded to sign a decree banning those newspapers and public meetings which were likely to attack the new authorities.

On 27 February, a week before polling day, the Reichstag building was burned down. A member of a left-wing group, Marinus van der Lubbe, was later convicted of setting it alight and was sentenced to death. It has sometimes been suggested that it was really the Nazis who started the fire, but it is now known that this was not so. The Nazis had been looking for an excuse to increase their power, and when a left-winger burned the Reichstag they made the most of it. Hitler claimed that the Reichstag fire showed that there was an immediate danger of a Bolshevik revolution. He issued a presidential decree 'for the Protection of the People and the State', which suspended indefinitely freedom of the press, freedom of speech, and freedom to hold meetings. 'Special' (which meant political) prisoners could be held for any period of time in 'protective custody' without being brought before a court. This decree remained till 1945 one of the foundations of the Nazi dictatorship.

It does not seem that when Hitler became chancellor, the Nazis had a carefully worked out plan to set up a dictatorship. In fact much of the violence against political opponents was the spontaneous reaction of grass-roots Nazis. We have seen that leading Nazis encouraged what they called 'the revolution from below', but it often got out of control and sometimes embarrassed the leaders. What Hitler did very effectively was ruthlessly to exploit to his advantage circumstances as they developed. The decree 'for the Protection of the People and the State' is a classic example of this.

What Hitler did plan from the outset on 30 January was Reichstag elections. When these took place a week after the Reichstag fire, the Nazis still got less than half the votes (44 per cent). Even with the help of his nationalist allies, Hitler still did not have the two thirds majority he needed to change the Weimar constitution by passing an Enabling Act to give him full powers. In the event he was given this by the support of Zentrum, which was concerned to safeguard the right of Catholics to worship in the new Germany. And everything was done to intimidate the deputies on the day the vote for the Enabling Act was taken (23 March). An SPD deputy described the scene:

> 'The wide square in front of the Kroll Opera House [where the Reichstag was meeting as a result of the fire] was crowded with dark masses of people. We were received with wild choruses: "We want the Enabling Act!" Youths with swastikas on their chests eyed us insolently, blocked our way, in fact made us run the gauntlet, calling us names like "Centre Pig", "Marxist Sow". The Kroll Opera House was crawling with armed SA men. The assembly hall was decorated with swastikas. When we Social Democrats had taken our seats on the extreme left, SA men lined up at the exits and along the walls behind us in a semicircle. Their expressions boded no good.
>
> We tried to dam the flood of Hitler's unjust accusations with interruptions of "No!", "An error!", "False!". But that did us no good. The SA hissed loudly and murmured: "Shut Up!", "Traitors!", "You'll be strung up today!".'

It said much for the courage of the SPD deputies that they alone voted against the Enabling Act, and even more for that of their chairman Otto Wells, who spoke this dignified and brave obituary for German democracy:

> 'We German Democrats pledge ourselves solemnly in this historic hour to the principle of humanity and justice, of freedom and socialism. No enabling act can give you the power to destroy ideas which are eternal and indestructible.'

The Enabling Act authorised the government to issue laws and decrees on its own authority. Unlike the decrees issued under Section 48 of the Weimar Constitution, the signature of the president was no longer needed, and laws and decrees could no longer be overturned by the Reichstag. Hitler made it appear that this had been decided legally.

The Weimar Republic was never formally abolished, but in reality it was now quite dead, and a Nazi dictatorship had been established.

ESSAY

Choose one of the following views about the rise of Hitler and the Nazis, and write an essay to discuss it.

1. 'Without Hitler the Nazis would have been another of the many extreme nationalist groups in Germany in the 1920s and would never have built up a mass support or come to power.'

2. 'The Nazis would have remained a small minority and Hitler would never have come to power had it not been for the Great Depression.'

3. 'Hitler could never have come to power and set up the Nazi dictatorship had his right-wing allies not underestimated him and had his left-wing enemies not been so seriously divided.'

The Nazi state, 1933–39

The day after he was appointed chancellor in January 1933 Hitler issued an 'Appeal to the German People.' He painted a lurid picture of how fourteen years of the republic had weakened Germany, for which he held 'Marxists' (the Social Democrats) responsible. Now, he argued, the communists were threatening to take over and destroy Germany entirely. This is how he put it:

'Over fourteen years have passed since that unhappy day [Armistice Day, 1918] when the German people, blinded by promises made by those at home and abroad, forgot the highest values of our past, of the Reich, of its honour and freedom, and thereby lost everything. Since these days of Treason, the Almighty has withdrawn his blessing from our nation. Discord and hatred have moved in. Filled with the deepest distress, millions of the best German men and women from all walks of life see the unity of the nation disintegrating... As so often in our history, Germany since the day the revolution broke out presents a picture of heartbreaking disunity...

All around us are symptoms portending breakdown. With an unparalleled effort of will and of brute force the Communist method of madness is trying as a last resort to poison and undermine an inwardly shaken and uprooted nation... Starting with the family, and including all notions of honour and loyalty, nation and fatherland, even the eternal foundations of our morals and our faith – nothing is spared by this negative, totally destructive ideology. Fourteen years of Marxism have undermined Germany. One year of Bolshevism would destroy Germany...

It is an appalling inheritance which we are taking over.

The task before us is the most difficult which has faced German statesmen in living memory. But we all have unbounded confidence, for we believe in our nation and its eternal values. Farmers, workers, and the middle class must unite to contribute the bricks wherewith to build the new Reich...

In place of our turbulent instincts, it will make national discipline govern our life.'

How would the new government defeat the Bolshevik threat? How would it restore 'national discipline'? How would it build a new Germany and make it respected in the world? We have already seen how the Nazis established the foundations of their dictatorship in the two months after Hitler became chancellor. The methods and the justifications continued along similar lines. Our study of how the Nazi state developed till 1939 and how it met the ambitions of its supporters can be divided into a number of issues:

1. How did Hitler and the Nazis consolidate their power in the period after the passing of the Enabling Act in March 1933? Did they create a 'monolithic state' as they hoped to do? How far was the survival of the Nazi state due to fear among its citizens?

2. What part did Hitler and his government play in bringing about economic recovery in Germany?

3. How far did the Nazis keep the support of the middle and upper classes by meeting their needs and how far by propaganda? How far did the Nazis alter the structure of society by replacing officials from the traditional ruling class by new Nazi officials from the lower middle class?

4. How far did the Nazis win the support of workers by giving them secure jobs and good leisure facilities?

5. How far did the Nazi youth organisations succeed in winning the support of young people?

6. Was the persecution of the Jews an essential aspect of the Nazi state or were the Jews simply convenient scapegoats in the attempt to unify other Germans?

7. Was Hitler's aggressive foreign policy an essential part of a plan for world domination or only a logical development of traditional German policy?

These issues raise questions about the *ideology* and *authority* of Hitler and the Nazis, and the sense of *identity* of the German people.

TASK

Put yourself in the place of German students of your age today. You are studying the Nazi state, and discussing whether it will be important to keep its lessons in mind when planning the reunified Germany of the 1990s and of the early twenty-first century.

Half the class will collect evidence which suggests that Hitler kept power because many Germans either agreed with him or were at least willing to go along with his aims. You do not believe that there is any danger of another brutal dictatorship appearing. On the other hand, you do think that the powerful German state which is emerging now will have to be careful to avoid some of the attitudes of the Nazis – particularly towards the outside world.

The other half of the class will collect evidence which suggests that Hitler was able to rule Germany only by a combination of propaganda and terror. You think that most Germans did not really support him, but were tricked or frightened into going along with his plans (the worst excesses of which they never knew). For these reasons you do not think modern Germans have any need to feel guilty about the Nazi period. Nor do you think there is any danger that the new Germany could become an aggressive state threatening the peace of Europe.

Hold a debate between those who support these two opposing points of view.

Take notes on the arguments of the opposing group.

Hitler's power
'Synchronisation'

The Nazis used the powers given by the Enabling Act of March 1933 to dispose of any organisation which might oppose or obstruct them, and to ensure that people in positions of authority supported them. This process was called 'Synchronisation'. One historian of modern Germany, V. R. Berghan, explains it in this way:

> 'He [Hitler] proceeded to establish a dictatorial regime of his own which obliterated, step by step, all constitutional and organisational obstacles in the way . . . Thus the political landscape of Germany was completely transformed within the following 15 months, and a regime was established which remained without parallel as far as its all-pervasive brutality and ruthlessness are concerned.'
>
> (*Modern Germany*)

The political parties

First to go were naturally the left-wing parties and the trade unions which supported them. The trade unions were banned by decree on 2 May 1933 and the Social Democratic Party, which had founded the Weimar Republic, on 22 June. There was no need to ban the Communist Party officially as its members were either dead, in concentration camps, in hiding, or had fled abroad. Most of the middle class and right-wing parties (even the ones which were supposed to be Hitler's allies in the government) dissolved themselves more or less willingly in June. The last party which held out was the Centre Party, which dissolved itself (rather unwillingly) on 5 July. These comments by one of its members show that it felt that it had no chance against the power of the Nazis, and in any case it partly accepted the need for special measures:

> 'Would it have been of any use to call on the Catholic population and the whole Centre Party to offer united resistance? Such resistance would have at once shown up the physical powerlessness of the party and would have been brutally suppressed; the leaders would have immediately been taken into "protective custody" and so been made harmless...
>
> It really was not possible to go on any further without force and since the Centre does not believe in this it could not complain if it were pushed aside. Therefore, it is right to let the new men, particularly the leaders of the National Socialists, go ahead and not put unnecessary obstacles in their way. There are a lot of dubious things in the National Socialist movement, particularly so far as principles are concerned. But that has to be put up with for the time being. Today there is no point in being fussy about legal subtleties. What matters is first to let a strong, efficient government grow and then to support it wholeheartedly to suppress Bolshevism.'

On 14 July the Nazi Party was decreed to be the only legal political party. Everything was now done to suggest that the Nazis and the new Germany were one and the same thing. Figure 8.1 illustrates this. It shows a rally at Nuremberg in September 1933. Nazi flags surround the podium from which Hitler is about to speak and ranks of supporters give him the Nazi salute.

It had not been necessary to use the power to issue decrees to get rid of most of the rival parties. For all but the left-wing parties it was enough that the power was there, and that many believed that there was indeed a communist danger and that the Nazis were best able to deal with it.

Reorganisation of the professions

During the same months the same factors led to the professions speedily being 'synchronised'. The professional organisations of doctors, lawyers, university and school teachers were reorganised under Nazi leaders, and more and more men in these professions became members of the Nazi party. By 1936 32 per cent of school teachers and 45 per cent of doctors were Nazis. No doubt some

Fig 8.1   A rally in Nuremberg in September 1933.

joined merely to improve their chances of promotion, but many in these professions genuinely believed that more respect for authority was needed. Those who did not believe this at least kept quiet through a very natural concern to protect their families.

The same applied to members of the civil service. A civil servant wrote this letter resigning from the SPD on 9 March (before it was banned):

'As a civil servant I have to make a choice. On the one hand, I see how the tendency is growing on the part of my employer, the Reich, not to tolerate those employees belonging to anti-Government associations. On the other hand, there is my loyalty to the Party. Unfortunately, I see no other solution but my resignation. The existence of my family is at stake. If the fate of unemployment, which in my experience can be very, very hard, is unavoidable, I need not reproach myself for having done everything in the interests of my wife and child.'

As this man pointed out, the decision was made easier by the general feeling that the Nazis were so ruthless and powerful that resistance was hopeless. He was right to be worried. In February and March 1933 local Nazis appeared in government offices as part of the 'revolution from below' and dismissed on the spot officials they believed to be left-wing. On 7 April the government made the process more orderly by issuing the 'Law for the Re-establishment of the Professional Civil Service'. It certainly wanted to get rid of political opponents, but it also needed an efficient civil service. The law laid down regulations for the dismissal of civil servants who were known opponents of the Nazis or who were Jews. (President Hindenburg insisted on a clause that Jews should not be dismissed if they had fought at the front or if their fathers or sons had been killed in the war). However, as in other professions, many civil servants were far from being enemies of the Nazis. Many had resented what they regarded as interference by Reichstag deputies during the Weimar Republic and thought that their power would be restored under a new authoritarian government. In any case, German civil servants had a tradition of doing things 'by the book' and tended to accept the Nazi dictatorship as legal because it was based on an act passed by the Reichstag.

The abolition of the state governments

The SA and other local Nazis who stormed into government offices during the 'revolution from below' dismissed, among many others, the leaders of the state governments. 'Reich Governors', usually the leading local Nazis, were appointed instead in April 1933. Like other German right-wingers, the Nazis really wanted to abolish the state governments as set up by Bismarck and to concentrate all power in Berlin. This was formally done in January 1934, when the special rights of the states were ended and their administrations came under the direct control of the Reich Government. Only Prussia remained in theory a separate state – not because of its size, but for a reason which was to become characteristic of the Nazi way of doing things. Its prime minister was Hermann Göring, one of Hitler's closest cronies, and the Führer was unwilling to refuse his pleas to save it.

The churches

At first it seemed that the Nazis had also succeeded in preventing opposition from the German churches. The Roman Catholic Church made an agreement (called a 'concordat') with the German government in July 1933. The church agreed that the Centre Party should be dissolved and that priests should not take part in political activities. In return, the church was promised that bishops would be allowed to communicate freely with Rome and to issue pastoral letters to their people. Religious orders and church schools would be allowed to continue.

Hitler had less respect for the power of the Protestant churches because they were divided. They were 'synchronised' in a more direct way by being put under the control of a 'Reichsbishop', who dismissed ministers opposed to the Nazis.

At first it seemed that Hitler had succeeded in getting his way with the churches as with other spheres of German life. However, their resistance soon started to grow. The Catholic bishops began to complain that the Nazis were breaking the terms of the concordat. In 1937 the Pope openly condemned Nazism. Many brave German priests did so also and by 1939 hundreds of them were in concentration camps. The Nazis were in time able to control all public Protestant organisations and church buildings. Many church-goers were either unconcerned or did not notice any difference. However, other Protestants followed the lead of Martin Niemoller (a First World War submarine commander and now a minister). They refused to use the official churches and held their own services. By the late 1930s these services had to be in secret and many people were sent to concentration camps for attending them.

The SA

Hitler would not tolerate anything (even in the Nazi camp) which threatened his own position or authority. By 1934 the SA was threatening both. The Nazi storm-troopers were now a huge organisation of 2,500,000 men under an ambitious and semi-independent leader, Ernst Röhm. The SA had been in the front line of the 'revolution from below', the reign of terror against the opponents of the Nazis in 1933. Although he sometimes tried to prevent this going too far, Hitler had really encouraged it to help clear the way for the Nazi dictatorship. It has often been said that after the failure of the 1923 coup Hitler decided that the Nazis must at least appear to gain power by legal means. It is true that his power to issue decrees was based on the Enabling Act passed by the Reichstag. However, he was quite unconcerned that most of the attacks carried out by the SA in 1933 when the Nazis were winning power were completely illegal.

By 1934 the SA seemed a threat to many people whom Hitler did not wish to offend. SA members felt aggrieved and restive because they believed more of them should have been given good jobs in return for their services. The civil service complained that they were bursting into offices and interfering with the business being done. More seriously, the army complained that the SA wanted to take over its functions within Germany, leaving it only to guard the frontiers. The army was the one part of the state which had not been 'synchronised'. Partly this was because the generals had right-wing opinions and were happy with Hitler's promise to restore the power of Germany in the world. Partly it was because the army was the only organisation with the power to overthrow the Nazis if it wished to do so. In the summer of 1934 Hitler was particularly keen to keep the goodwill of the army commanders. It was clear that President Hindenburg was nearing death. Hitler wanted to issue a decree proclaiming himself the new president and commander-in-chief. If the army agreed to this it would mean that every soldier would swear an oath of loyalty to him personally. As the traditional code of honour was very important in the German army, this would be a great prize. It was much too important to be endangered by the undisciplined behaviour and delusions of grandeur of the SA. The days were numbered, therefore, for the independent power of the SA and also for the lives of many of its leaders.

On what became known as 'The Night of the Long Knives', Hitler showed that the ruthlessness which was the fundamental feature of his dictatorship could be turned against Nazis as well as against open opponents.

Hitler ordered a meeting of SA leaders for 30 June 1934 at Wiessee, near Munich. He flew from Berlin in the middle of the night in order to be able to carry out the arrests personally. Röhm and his colleagues were dragged from their beds. Hitler went round either ordering their arrest or (in a few cases) telling them to go. Röhm and several of the other SA leaders were executed in Munich. The remainder were taken to Berlin, where Göring was in charge of disposing of them. A police officer who was there later gave this account:

'Through the door we can see Göring and his colleagues putting their heads together. Occasionally we hear an inarticulate sound like "Off!" or "Aha!" or "Shoot!" or simply raucous laughter. In any case they don't seem to be in a bad mood. Göring even exudes an air of well-fed comfort. He gives the impression of being in his element. He strides round his room.

Suddenly things begin to get very noisy. Police Major Jakobi rushes out of the room in great haste. Göring's hoarse voice booms after him: "Shoot them down . . . Shoot at once!" One can't begin to describe the blatant bloodthirstiness, the savage fury, the hideous vindictiveness, and yet at the same time the terror shown in this scene. Everyone senses, Someone has escaped who must not be allowed to escape, someone whose escape will undo the whole day's work.'

Most of the SA leaders and some of the ordinary members were murdered. The opportunity was also taken to kill other Nazis who were seen as troublemakers and some important non-Nazis against whom they bore a grudge.

Hitler got what he wanted from 'The Night of the Long Knives'. When Hindenburg died on 2 August the Führer became president as well as chancellor. The SA was much reduced in size and influence. Apart from Hitler, the principal gainer was Heinrich Himmler. He had been one of those in Göring's room and his police and SS forces had helped with the arrests and carried out the executions. This was an important moment in the development of Germany as a police state under Himmler's supervision.

A police state

The SS began in 1925 as a personal guard for Hitler. When Himmler became its commander in 1929 it was built up into an élite force within the SA. It had a distinctive black uniform and, unlike the SA, was strictly disciplined. By 1934 it had 50,000 members. However, this was only one part of Himmler's power base. In 1933 he won control of the secret police of most of the states and in 1934 was in the process of taking over from Göring the Prussian secret police (the Geheime Staatspolizei or Gestapo). For its services on 30 June 1934 the SS was made an independent organisation outside the SA, answerable only to Himmler and to Hitler himself. It rapidly grew to become a large and powerful force.

Himmler was, therefore, in charge of the SS and the secret police, and over the next two years acquired the power of arresting whoever he wished (subject only to Hitler's instructions). This was formalised in 1936 when he became chief of German police and the criminal branch was merged with the secret police. Himmler and his deputy, Reinhard Heydrich, ran the police state which many people later claimed had frightened them into going along with Hitler's policies.

The concentration camps

Himmler's power was certainly fearsome. He controlled the Gestapo, which could arrest 'special prisoners' (opponents of the Nazis). He also ran (through the SS) the concentration camps where they were kept under 'protective custody.' Hundreds of thousands of Germans were sent without trial to concentration camps. Some were later released, but others died in the camps. The camps were modelled on the one Himmler had set up at Dachau in Bavaria in 1933. These extracts from the Dachau regulations shows how brutally prisoners were treated in concentration camps:

'Tolerance means weakness. Punishment will be mercilessly handed out whenever the interests of the fatherland warrant it. The fellow countryman who is decent but misled will never be affected by these regulations. But let it be a warning both to the inciting politicians and to intellectual agitators; watch out that you are not caught, for otherwise it will be your neck.

ARTICLE 6. The following are punishable with eight days' solitary confinement and twenty-five strokes administered before and after the serving of the sentence:

Anyone making uncomplimentary or ironical remarks to a member of the SS, deliberately omitting the prescribed marks of respect, or in some other way demonstrating unwillingness to submit himself to disciplinary measures.

ARTICLE 7. The following are punishable with two weeks' solitary confinement: Anyone smoking in shelters, toilets and places which are fire hazards.

ARTICLE 11. In accordance with the law on revolutionaries, the following offenders, considered as agitators, will be hanged. Anyone who, for the purpose of agitating, does the following in the camp: discusses politics, carries on controversial talks and meetings, collects true or false information about the camp or smuggles such information out of the camp.'

In addition to being sent without trial to the camps, Germans could also be tried in court for minor 'political offences', such as making uncomplimentary remarks about the government. On one day in 1939 there were 162,734 people in 'protective custody' (which means without trial) and 112,432 who had been convicted of opposition.

In Nazi Germany the entire process of law and imprisonment was manipulated by the Nazis for their own ends. This would have been much more difficult had most judges and lawyers not accepted that their duty was to carry out the Führer's wishes. The legal profession was one of those which had been 'synchronised', and in 1936 the head of the association of Nazi lawyers issued this statement about what was expected of judges:

'1. It is not the duty of a judge to enforce a law superior to the national community or to impose a system of universal values. His role is to safeguard the racial community, to eliminate dangerous elements, to prosecute all acts harmful to the community, and to arbitrate in disagreements between members of the community.
2. The National Socialist ideology, especially as expressed in the party programme and in the speeches of our Führer, is the basis for interpreting the law.
3. The judge has no right to scrutinise decisions made by the Führer and issued in the form of a law or decree. The judge is also bound by any other decisions of the Führer which clearly lay down what people should do.'

This meant that the law was there, not to enforce a long-established code of what was right or wrong, but to carry out the instructions of the government. For any judge who was not in sympathy with this, there were various pressures to make him comply. In the last resort he would be dismissed.

Many claimed later that they had been terrorised into accepting Hitler's rule by the threat of the concentration camps and the knowledge that they would not get a fair trial. However, research by historians has shown that some sections of the community were much more likely than others to suffer from Hitler and Himmler's police state. For example, Ian Kershaw has written that:

> 'If we confine our attention to Germany itself . . . terror and repression were highly selective in their application. Workers associated with left-wing parties were thrown into concentration camps in their thousands, especially during the initial onslaught in 1933. Industrialists, landowners (till 1944) and bankers were left untouched. Jews, an unloved minority, were terrorised . . . Police harassment was far more prevalent in working class than in middle class areas of big cities. There was no assault on the farming and small property-holding population of the countryside. There was no army purge in the early years. Most intellectuals [such as writers, scientists and university teachers], apart from the minority forced to emigrate, needed no terror to make them fall into line with Nazi 'co-ordination'. . . Generally, then, repression was aimed at the powerless and unpopular sections of society.'
>
> (*Hitler*)

It seems that the large number of Germans who were inclined to support (or at least to give the benefit of the doubt to) the Führer did not have reason to be in real fear. For them concentration camps were places where other people were sent – the sort of people of whom they usually disapproved. It is clear that the secret police got a lot of support from members of the public. It was they who denounced a large number of the people dealt with by the Gestapo. There were simply not enough secret policemen to hunt them all out themselves. For example, Düsseldorf in 1937 had about half a million people and only 126 Gestapo officers. We have already seen why many Germans welcomed Hitler in 1933 and we will consider later why many continued to accept him.

'Führer state'

It used to be thought that Hitler set up not only a police state which terrorised all its people, but a monolithic state in which all power was concentrated in his hands – one in which all important decisions were taken at the top and passed down in a very organised way. This is what is suggested by the phrase 'Führer state' which Nazis often used. In fact the government of Germany was less organised than it had been under the empire or even under the republic. The old administration survived, but in many matters decisions were not carried out through it but through the organisations controlled by individual Nazi leaders. Himmler's SS/Gestapo empire was the most powerful of these. Other important ones were controlled by Göring (Prussia, the air force, and later the economy) and Goebbels (propaganda). Often even these Nazi organisations were not carrying out the Führer's direct orders. Of course they all knew in general terms what he wanted and they sought to do it. They called this 'working towards the Führer', and it was expected of everyone in Germany.

One of the ways in which Hitler's authority was built up was that after 1933 he always appeared in public in uniform (see Figure 8.2), which since the days of the empire had been a way to win respect in Germany.

If Hitler was interested in a particular matter and gave a detailed order it would be carried out without question. However, as a rule Hitler liked to let his leading supporters (and the organisations they controlled) battle out the details among themselves. He preferred not to spend long hours working out detailed policies. If there were no obvious winners in the battles between his supporters, he would decide. The top Nazis at least saw him regularly and could get his opinion. However, ministers who were not so close to Hitler could find it very difficult to get a decision from him. One official described how he worked:

> 'Hitler did not love Berlin. Mostly he was in Berchtesgaden [in Bavaria]. There was no such thing as a Government with Cabinet meetings. Ministers in charge of departments might for months on end, and even for years, have no opportunity of speaking to Hitler... Anything that could not be settled between departments on their own account was referred to Berchtesgaden in order that it might be brought to Hitler's attention. Sometimes the matter was simply put aside as 'pending'. Ministerial skill consisted in making the most of a favourable hour or minute when Hitler made a decision, this often taking the form of remark thrown out casually, which then went its way as an "Order of the Führer".'

The Nazi state was monolithic in the sense that all officials were expected to follow Hitler's ideas and to carry out his orders, but it was not a state in which all the orders were made at the top and passed down in a clear and organised way.

Hitler and the economy

When Hitler came to power in 1933 in the depths of the Depression, one of his most powerful promises was to get Germany back to work. This table shows how far that was achieved.

Fig 8.2 Hitler in uniform shortly after becoming chancellor.

	Germany	
	Index of industrial production	Unemployment (Annual average percentage)
1928	100	6.3
1929	102	8.5
1930	84	14.0
1931	62	21.9
1932	58	29.9
1933	66	25.9
1934	83	13.5
1935	96	10.3
1936	107	7.4
1937	117	4.1
1938	125	1.9
1939	132	0.5

These figures show that in 1936 output overtook what it had been in 1929 (the peak of the Weimar boom); and in 1939 it was twice the level at which it had been when the Nazis took over in 1933. And unemployment dropped steadily from nearly a third of the workforce in 1932 to almost nothing in 1939. In fact in 1939 there were labour shortages in many areas.

Some historians have argued that, as all countries were recovering from the Depression from the mid-1930s, Hitler cannot claim the credit for this economic recovery. But there is no doubt that Germany recovered faster than countries like the USA, Britain and France. Reparations payments had been completely ended in 1932 because of the Depression (as Bruning had hoped). However, they had not been heavy enough to make that much difference. Other historians suggest that Hitler and his economics minister, Schacht, carried out first what came later to be accepted by almost every other country for the next forty-odd years – that the best way to get out of a depression is for the government to spend money and to forget about balancing the books. It is certainly true that the German government's debts rose sharply after 1933, as unemployment dropped. It is also true that there were job creation schemes, the most famous being the motorways (called 'Autobahns') which were built across Germany. Figure 8.3 shows Hitler opening one of them. (Although the Nazis got the

Fig 8.3   Hitler opening a new Autobahn.

maximum publicity from these schemes, they had actually been started under the previous government. Significantly, the main change made by Hitler was to insist that the Autobahn network must make it possible for the army to move quickly between the western and eastern frontiers.)

It seems clear now that the German economy recovered so fast because Hitler started rearming as soon as he came to power. This had to be camouflaged at first as it was contrary to the terms of the Treaty of Versailles and Hitler was still trying to persuade other countries that his intentions were peaceful. Orders were placed with a limited number of firms to make it easier to keep them secret. Auto Union produced 'lorries' which were military vehicles, and Krupp had an 'agricultural tractor programme' which produced tanks. These programmes were under way in 1933. A large explosives firm more than doubled its workforce in the first half of 1933. New warships were ordered. In 1934 almost half of the aeroplanes produced were military ones (which Germany was not supposed to have).

Göring said later that the Nazis insisted on 'guns before butter'. This was an oversimplification. Imports of food remained at a high level to ensure that people did not go short. The output figures show that the production of consumer goods increased, but not nearly as fast as the production of war materials. By 1936 it was clear to those in charge of Germany's economy that the sums were not adding up. Despite the great increases in government borrowing, Germany was finding it difficult to buy all the raw materials she needed from abroad for her rearmament programme.

Hitler put Göring in charge of a new 'Four Year Plan' and wrote for him a very detailed memorandum outlining the options and giving him instructions. He set Göring two basic tasks:

'I. The German armed forces must be operational within four years.
II. The German economy must be fit for war within four years.'

Hitler made it clear again and again in this document that the first priority was to prepare for war (and references to the Bolshevik threat show that he saw Russia as the enemy). Although it would be expensive, more food should be grown at home. This would free foreign exchange to buy raw materials for making weapons. One way or another, the food supply must be kept up so that the people would be in good condition to fight the war. The most important thing of all was to build up Germany's stocks of weapons. Because of the shortage of foreign exchange, Germany must use more of her own low-grade iron ore and increase production of synthetic rubber and oil. This would also be very expensive, but it must be done as Germany could not otherwise be prepared for war.

In this document Hitler made clear that he did not have original and enlightened ideas for getting the Germans back to work. What the Nazis were doing was deliberately to distort the economy to prepare for war. In the short term this certainly created jobs, but it could only be paid for by enormous loans. If these could not be recouped from conquered countries, the German economy would be in serious trouble and the new jobs would disappear.

Hitler and the middle class

Although Nazism appealed to a wide range of people in Germany, there is no doubt that the bedrock of Hitler's support came from the middle class or from people who thought of themselves as middle class. We have seen that the police state recognised and depended on the support of such people. It was vital for Hitler to retain middle class support after he came to power.

Nazi propaganda

The Nazi propaganda machine played an important part in winning and retaining support. When Hitler became chancellor, Dr Joseph Goebbels was already recognised as the Nazis' propaganda genius. In March 1933 he became the head of a new Ministry of Popular Enlightenment and Propaganda, and co-ordinated the Nazi message and the methods by which it was spread. He continued organising mass rallies. The marching columns and the emotional speeches gave those who attended a feeling of elation and involvement. The most famous were the annual Nuremberg rallies. Figure 8.4 gives an idea of the impressive pageants which Goebbels staged.

Now that the Nazis were in power they had also to put their message over daily, and to the entire nation. It was only gradually that most newspapers were brought under direct government control through ownership by the Nazi publishing house. However, from October 1933 papers could be closed or editors dismissed if they offended the government. As radio was already state-run, it was much easier to control. Goebbels was concious of the value of radio in getting the Nazi message into people's homes. Radio ownership was encouraged by selling cheap sets and by 1939, 70 per cent of German households had radios (– this was more than anywhere else in the world). Goebbels was also enthusiastic about the propaganda value of films and took a close interest in film-making techniques. He was most successful in making documentary films, such as of the Nuremberg rallies and the Berlin Olympic Games of 1936 (a great propaganda triumph for the Nazis). These instructions for a film of Hitler's fiftieth birthday celebrations in 1939 illustrate the careful planning to get the maximum propaganda value:

Fig 8.4 The 1938 Nuremberg rally.

'Under a bright, shining sky the birthday itself begins. Cheerful marching tunes resound; the SS give Hitler a birthday serenade. Surrounded by some of his co-workers, among whom Himmler stands out, Hitler receives the homage. The camera lingers lovingly on the Goebbels children, all clothed in white, who stand, curious but well behaved, next to Hitler, thus strengthening his reputation as a true lover of children – a special shot for women in the audience. Now the picture turns to the crowd. A gigantic chorus in front of the Reich Chancellery swells in a song of jubilation for Hitler. Now Hitler appears on the balcony before the crowd, which breaks out into a repeated ovation.'

It has sometimes been said that Nazi propaganda treated people as unintelligent and gullible. However, the evidence is that while the Nazis were in power (as during their rise) their propaganda succeeded best with people who were already inclined to accept the message. Many middle class Germans accepted it because Hitler had come to power to do things that they thought were needed and because they felt they were benefiting under his rule.

These extracts from the diary of a well-to-do lady in Hamburg, Frau Solmitz, show that, while she had reservations about Hitler, she thought that he was needed to deal with the 'Bolshevik threat':

> 30/1/33. Hitler is Chancellor of the Reich! And what a Cabinet! One we didn't dare dream of in July. Hitler, Hugenberg, Seldte, Papen!!!
>
> On each one of them depends part of Germany's hopes ... It is so incredibly marvellous that I am writing it down quickly before the first discordant note comes.
> 6/2/33. Torchlight procession of National Socialists and Stalhelm [another right-wing group]! A wonderfully elevating experience for all of us ... On Sunday the Reds marched through relentless rain, with wives and children to make the procession longer. The Socialists and Reds will inevitably have to give in now.
> 7/2/33. Hitler's appeal, signed by the whole Government, contains too many foreign words used in an uneducated way. But I say: let him act first, and then later we shall teach Hitler good, pure German.'

The last extract reflects the feeling of some middle and most upper class Germans that the Nazis were vulgar and uneducated. Such people were probably shocked when Hitler pushed aside his right-wing allies and set-up a Nazi dictatorship. On the other hand, he also got rid of the left-wing parties and the trade unions. The fear of a communist revolution had been banished. The economy was recovering and businesses were doing well, whether you were a small shopkeeper or the owner of a great engineering firm or steelworks. Civil service and other professional salaries were increasing in value. German nationalists were proud to see Germany playing a more prominent part in the world. If you were either an industrialist or an officer in the armed forces, you welcomed rearmament. Your family and the people you knew did not feel they were in danger of being arrested or sent to a concentration camp.

Ian Kershaw has summed up why many middle and upper class Germans were inclined to accept Nazi propaganda (even if not always wholeheartedly):

> 'All the currents of opinion which Goebbels was able to tap, articulate and reinforce, flowed together in the feeling that there must be a new start for Germany, a national rebirth. The very depths of division nurtured the longing for unity which found resonance in Nazi slogans of a "national Community". The politicians' bickerings in a weak and fragmented democracy heightened belief in the virtues of strong, authoritarian, "law and order" government. The fears of Marxism widely prevalent among the German middle and upper classes ... offered the prospect of instant approval for any government which could remove such fears once and for all. The national humiliation

and fury at the post-war treatment of Germany by the victorious Allies, and anxiety about the nation's future fostered the readiness to acclaim a bold foreign policy asserting Germany's rights from a position of military strength. Not least, any government which could rescue Germany from the depths of economic collapse and offer the hope of a new and lasting prosperity could reckon with support which overcome party political rivalries.'

(*Hitler*)

When the Nazis came to power it seemed likely that they would please particularly the lower middle class. They said that they would alter the structure of society by replacing officials from the traditional ruling class by new Nazi officials from the lower middle class. What was needed was a new 'Volkish' community in which it would be 'leadership of men' which was rewarded. Senior jobs should be given to those who had struggled to the top by means of their own qualities instead of to those who had been appointed in the past because of their money or family connections.

It is certainly true that many Nazis got official jobs during the 'revolution from below' in 1933. Since the SA had played a large part in forcing out old officials, its members often replaced them, and they were usually from lower middle class families (such as small shopkeepers or self-employed craftsmen). Some of these men rose to high positions in the Nazi state, but they certainly did not sweep away the traditional ruling class. In fact, one of the reasons for the unrest in the SA in 1934 was that its members thought they were not getting enough senior jobs in industry or in government service.

Throughout the 1930s a factory manager was still most likely to be from a family of wealthy businessmen. A senior civil servant was still most likely to be from a family of civil servants and to have gone to university. Senior army officers were still most likely to have come from landowning families. Even the leaders of the Nazi élite force, the SS, were often from the educated middle class. For example, Himmler's deputy Heydrich had been a naval officer and his father had been the head of a college of music. Heydrich encouraged the appointment of men of his own sort.

Historians have tried to find out why more lower middle class Nazis were not appointed to top positions. One reason was that many of the existing holders of these jobs joined the Nazi Party and were then more difficult to dismiss. By 1937 63 per cent of public servants were party members. Some no doubt did this to save their jobs, but, as we have seen on page 176, a large number of them sympathised with many of the things that Hitler was trying to do. In any case Hitler found that he needed the help of trained and experienced officials to run the country.

Hitler and the workers

Workers were less likely than middle or upper class Germans to be sympathetic to Goebbels's propaganda machine. They were most likely to belong to the trade unions and left-wing parties which Hitler campaigned against and in 1933 forcibly closed down. Their friends and relations were more likely to have been arrested or killed in the reign of terror against the left in 1933. Throughout the 1930s they had more reason to fear the knock on the door by the Gestapo officer who would take them off to a concentration camp. It is true that they were also much more likely to have a regular job than during the Depression years. But, although their working hours were lengthened, they did not see any real increase in the value of their wages. This was in marked contrast to most professional people and officials.

The Nazis did try to win the support of manual workers. After trade unions were banned in 1933, workers were obliged to join instead the German Labour Front and to pay contributions to it. Unlike a trade union, this did not bargain with employers over wages. However, it did allow workers to press for such things as better lighting, ventilation and canteens. It also gave them access to the leisure activities of the 'Strength Through Joy' movement, which organised theatre outings, sports, excursions, hikes, holidays, and even ocean cruises for workers. 'Strength Through Joy' was understandably popular, and in 1938 over nine million people took part in its activities. But it does not seem to have won large-scale working class support for the Nazis, as had been hoped.

It is difficult to calculate the amount of working class opposition to Hitler. It was too dangerous to criticise him openly. Although some of Hitler's young supporters were the children of Social Democrats, there is evidence that it was much more common for Social Democrats to pass on their beliefs to the next generation in private round the supper table. In public they would keep quiet. For example, Ernst Bromberg was a fitter in the Krupp steelworks at Essen. He voted SPD at every election up to 1933 and joined the SPD again after the war (when it revived to become an important party in the new democratic Germany). By around 1980 he was an old man and was interviewed for an oral history project. He made it clear that under the Nazis he had kept his head down. At that time he had nothing to do with 'the whole political business':

'No time for it, when you're on three shift working. People kicked against the Labour Front a bit later on and then it just carried on. Obviously if you were on piece work, you didn't have time to make any speeches. You got up in the morning when you had to; you didn't overstretch your break periods because, after all, the money was tempting. I didn't worry any more about the Nazis, put it that way, apart from my Labour

Front contribution. I just didn't have anything to do with the Nazis – and anyway I was tied up with my Protestant clubs all week [he was a keen member of the church choir]. Nothing really changed there.'

Many German workers, like Ernst Bromberg, were not persuaded by Nazi propaganda in the 1930s. They just kept their heads down and got on with earning a living, bringing up a family, and enjoying their hobbies.

Hitler and German youth

The Nazis made great efforts to win the support of young people and to create a new National Socialist generation. By 1936 it was compulsory to join one of the Nazi youth movements – for boys, the German Young People (from age ten to fourteen) and the Hitler Youth (from fourteen to eighteen) and for girls the League of Young Girls (from ten to fourteen) and the League of German Girls (from fourteen to eighteen). Their purpose was to create young Nazis and also to build a generation which was disciplined and fit for war. They were drilled in military-style parades and listened to political speeches. One member said later that:

'We were politically programmed – to stop thinking when the magic word "Fatherland" was uttered and Germany's honour and greatness were mentioned.'

A considerable number of the Hitler Youth did pass with enthusiasm at the age of eighteen into adult Nazi organisations. Figure 8.5 (page 192) shows a parade at which this happened.

The girls' organisations preached the Nazi belief that the place of German women was in the home. However, the youth movements were not all about parades and political preaching. The members also took part in many sports. They cycled, hiked and camped. For many, these movements took them among youngsters of their own age and away from the control of their homes and their parents in a way which had not been possible before. This was especially true in country areas and with girls (in curious contrast to the Nazi view of women). Figure 8.6 (page 192) shows girls parading Nazi flags before a gymnastics display – an activity which combined support for the party, discipline, and fitness.

It seems clear that the Nazi youth movements had considerable success in winning the support of young people and in preparing them for the tasks which would face them in war. On the other hand, like all Nazi propaganda, they had a greater effect on those whose background inclined them to be receptive. In the late 1930s youngsters were being forced in who had previously refused to join, and they were naturally less easily enthused. Even during the war, when German life was highly disciplined, working class

Fig 8.5   Members of
Hitler Youth being sworn
in as full members of the
party at the age of
eighteen.

Fig 8.6   Nazi girls on
parade.

youths in the industrialised areas of western Germany formed gangs called 'Edelweiss Pirates'. They had a special uniform, arranged their own unofficial activities such as hikes, and disliked the Hitler Youth so much that they would attack them whenever they had superior numbers.

Hitler and the Jews

Persecution of the Jews began very soon after Hitler came to power. As before, hatred of them was a major element in Nazi propaganda, but now it was featured prominently in practically all the media. Jews were among the groups which suffered at the hands of the SA thugs in the 'Revolution from below' in the spring of 1933. A boycott of Jewish shops was declared in some areas and people were warned not to use them. Figure 8.7 shows a large clothes store with 'Jew!' written on most of the windows.

Fig. 8.7   The Nazi boycott of Jewish shops: 'Jew!' is written on the windows of this store.

Figure 8.8 shows SA men posting notices such as 'It is forbidden to buy anything in this Jewish shop'. Some Jewish shops were destroyed, and Jews were beaten up and sent to concentration camps.

Fig 8.8   A Jewish shop in 1933.

In April 1933 the Law for the Re-establishment of the Professional Civil Service provided for the dismissal of Jews from public service. This introduced to the law the concept of 'non-Aryan' (meaning Jewish) descent. Jews were soon barred from teaching in universities and acting as court lawyers. It was made more difficult for them to practise as doctors.

It has sometimes been suggested that Hitler was using the Jews as convenient scapegoats to try to unify other Germans at a stage when this was a particularly important aim. In fact there is evidence that persecution of the Jews was limited for practical reasons during his early years in power. It was only later that he felt free to give full rein to the hatred of them which had always been an essential part of his political beliefs. Further persecution of the Jews was actually resisted by Hitler for a while. At this stage he wanted to keep the goodwill of public opinion abroad and was worried about damaging the recovery of business (in which Jews had always played an important part).

But in 1935 he felt able to go further. The Nuremberg Laws now effectively deprived Jews of German citizenship. These are some of the provisions:

'A citizen of the Reich may be only one who is of German or kindred blood.

Only the citizen of the Reich may enjoy full political rights.

A Jew cannot be a citizen of the Reich. He cannot exercise the right to vote; he cannot occupy public office.

A Jew is an individual who is descended from at least three grandparents who were racially full Jews.

Any marriages between Jews and citizens of German or kindred blood are herewith forbidden.

Jews are forbidden to employ as servants in their households female subjects of German or kindred blood who are under the age of 45 years.

Jews are prohibited from displaying the Reich and national flag and from showing the national colours.'

Persecution of the Jews now increased constantly. Jews were obliged to register as 'non-Aryan'. Their access to schools and universities was strictly limited. They had to register their assets. There was increasing pressure on employers to dismiss them.

The murder by a Jew of an official of the German embassy in Paris was used as an excuse for a new outbreak of violence against Jews. What was claimed to be a spontaneous outburst of anger happened in towns throughout Germany on the night of 7/8 November 1938. This became known as 'Kristallnacht' (the night of broken glass) because so many windows were broken. Everywhere the pattern was the same. The American consul in Leipzig described what happened there:

'At 3 a.m. was unleashed a barrage of Nazi ferocity as had had

no equal hitherto in Germany. Jewish buildings were smashed
into and contents demolished or looted. Jewish apartments have
been looted of cash, silver and jewellery.

Jewish shop windows by the hundreds were systematically
and wantonly smashed throughout the entire city. The main
streets of the city were a positive litter of plate glass. According
to reliable witnesses, this was done by SS men and Storm-
troopers not in uniform, each group having been provided with
hammers, axes, crowbars and fire bombs.

Three synagogues were fired simultaneously and no attempts
were made to put out the fires. They were all gutted. One of
the largest clothing stores was also gutted by fire. The firemen
did nothing to save it but sprayed surrounding buildings.

The most hideous phase of the so-called 'spontaneous' action
has been the wholesale arrest and transportation to
concentration camps of male German Jews between the ages of
16 and 60. This has been taking place daily since the night of
horror.'

It has been estimated that about a hundred Jews died that night
and that over 20,000 Jewish men were taken to concentration
camps. It was now obvious to all that the condition of German
Jews was worsening rapidly. Because we know of the terrible
tragedy which was to follow, it is easy for us to assume that this
was part of a carefully worked out programme for ridding
Germany of the Jews. In fact this did not exist in early November
1938. Kristallnacht was not spontaneous, but it had been organised
at short notice by a small group of Nazi leaders under Goebbels.
Göring, who was now in charge of the economy, was horrified
by the economic damage it did. He insisted that a more systematic
plan should be produced. It was only now that the state became
fully involved in getting rid of the Jews. From January 1939 they
were forbidden to run their own businesses or to mix with
Germans in housing or in many public places. What were they to
do? The state now encouraged them to emigrate. In 1939 the
number of Jews in Germany fell to 350,000 (from 515,000 in
1933).

The outbreak of war in September 1939 meant that the remaining Jews were trapped in Germany and also that in conquered
Poland the Nazis now ruled many more Jews. Matters moved
speedily towards Hitler's horrifying 'final solution' to the 'Jewish
problem'. From late 1939 Jews began to be deported from
Germany to Poland. With the invasion of Russia in 1941 Hitler
believed he was now involved in the titanic final struggle with
'Jewish Bolshevism' which he had long prophesied. As part of
this, huge numbers of Jews in the east were exterminated in the
gas chambers of concentration camps such as Auschwitz. It has
been estimated that between four and six million were killed by

the Nazis in what came to be known by Jews as 'The Holocaust'. This represented about half the Jewish population of Europe at the beginning of the war. It had not been carefully planned from the outset, but it was a terrible realisation of all the denunciations against the Jews and the promises of vengeance which Hitler had made over the years.

Hitler and German foreign policy

We have seen that from about 1923 Hitler had a world view which saw Germany re-establishing her national greatness through a great struggle in the east with 'Jewish Bolshevism'. He believed that the German population was becoming too large to support itself on German territory and must win new territory or living space ('Lebensraum') in Eastern Europe. This would be done in a struggle with what he saw as the two great threats to Germany – the Jews and the communists (and he believed these two were united in the Soviet Union).

As it was inevitable that great nations should struggle for mastery, he foresaw that eventually Germany would have to fight the maritime powers for world supremacy (or perhaps only the United States if he could make an alliance with Britain). In *Mein Kampf* he claimed that this was a totally new foreign policy for Germany:

> 'We must take our stand on the necessity of bringing our territorial area into just proportion with the number of our population. From the past we can learn only one lesson. And this is that the aim which we must pursue is twofold: namely (1) the acquisition of territory as the objective of our foreign policy and (2) the establishment of a new and uniform foundation for our political activities at home in accordance with our doctrine of nationhood.
>
> Therefore we National Socialists have purposely drawn a line through the type of conduct followed by pre-war Germany in foreign policy. We put an end to the perpetual Germanic march towards the south and west of Europe and turn our eyes towards the lands of the east. We finally put a stop to the colonial and trade policy of pre-war times and pass over to the territorial policy of the future. But when we speak of new territory in Europe today, we must principally think of Russia and the border states subject to her. Destiny itself seems to wish to point out the way for us here.'

The famous English historian A. J. P. Taylor wrote in the 1960s that these were just 'day dreams'; and he and others have argued that Hitler's foreign policy was really not very different from that of his predecessors. Their argument is as follows. Hitler took from Bismarck the model of a statesman as someone who strengthens his own country by immoral means. He followed in the footsteps of all his predecessors since 1871 in seeking to build up the greatness of Germany. Many other Germans had wished to control the lands to the east, and this had become official policy during the First World War. In September 1914 the chancellor, Bethmann-Hollweg, had made a statement of Germany's war aims. Lithuania (and if possible other lands on the east coast of the Baltic) would become German. There would be a new Polish state under German control. In addition he said:

> 'We must create a central European economic association through common customs treaties, to include France, Belgium, Holland, Denmark, Austria-Hungary, Poland and perhaps Italy, Sweden and Norway. This association will not have any constitutional supreme authority and all its members will be formally equal, but in practice will be under German leadership and must stabilise Germany's economic dominance over "Mitteleuropa" [Middle Europe].'

Germany showed her ambitions in the east in 1918 after the defeat of Russia. In the Treaty of Brest-Litovsk Russia lost Poland and part of the Baltic states. Before she was herself defeated, Germany had gained full control of some of the Baltic lands and was hoping that friendly governments would be set up in the other areas lost by Russia. A leading German historian, Fritz Fischer, has pointed out that in both the First and Second World Wars:

> 'Much as the aims may have differed in detail and in the means used to achieve them, one thing cannot be denied: the aim was, and the effect would have been, had Germany been victorious, the domination of the German Empire on the European continent.'

It is argued that even the Weimar governments which he so despised shared many of Hitler's foreign aims. They wanted to restore Germany's position in Europe and to overturn the more objectionable terms of the Treaty of Versailles, which were resented by almost all Germans. In particular they aimed to rebuild the armed forces, to win back lands lost in the east and to enable Germans outside the Reich (such as in Austria) to join it if they wished.

It is certainly true that Hitler shared some of the aims and attitudes of traditional German foreign policy. Many of his aims were commonplace among right-wing nationalist parties in Germany. Some of his views (especially on the Treaty of Versailles) were supported by a wide range of Germans. It was always Hitler's strength that he reflected many of the resentments and shared some of the hopes of a large number of his fellow countrymen.

However, his foreign policy went very much further than that of his predecessors, and in essential respects it was different in kind. Prior to him, official German ambitions had been at their highest during the First World War. These aims were government policy during a short period, and even then there was no thought of Germany taking over large amounts of land in the east. What Bethmann-Hollweg spoke of in 1914 and what was intended in 1918 was an economic community dominated by Germany. The states of eastern Europe would be influenced by Germany, but not directly ruled by her. Certainly no previous German leader would have contemplated using the populations of eastern Europe as slave labour and killing them in large numbers (as happened during the Second World War).

On the other hand, most historians would now agree that Hitler did not have a detailed plan of how he would dominate first Europe and then the world. It is difficult to look at *Mein Kampf* or at the speeches which he regularly made as Führer to his generals and find a blueprint which is reflected exactly in what he later did. Many people have tried to do this, but the parts never fit together. He did things in a different order from what he had prophesied. He did some things which he had not prophesied and which were a suprise to everyone. The truth seems to be that in foreign policy (as in his actions within Germany) he was an opportunist. It is clear from the great priority Hitler gave to rearming (which Germany could not afford from her own resources) that war was the likely result, and that he knew that. But how or even when it would happen he was not sure. He was skilful at spotting and exploiting the weaknesses of his enemies and taking advantage of events as they arose. This makes his policy seem unplanned and sometimes inconsistent. However, he was always working towards the same general goals he had set years before in *Mein Kampf*. This view has been summed up by V. R. Berghan:

> 'If one cuts through the diplomatic detail to be found in the files, a pattern can be seen which tallies with Hitler's writings of the 1920s. Throughout the 1930s, he kept his eyes firmly fixed on the acquisition of "living space" in the east, while trying to woo Britain into an alliance on the basis of a simple tit-for-tat: London was to acquiesce in Germany's violent expansion on the European continent in return for the Third Reich's co-operation in maintaining the British Empire overseas . . . When it became clear that Britain was not prepared to make a deal with Germany on these terms, this did not cause Hitler to abandon his European plans.'
>
> (*Modern Germany*)

All this can be seen from an examination of the successive moves Hitler made in foreign policy.

In May 1933 Hitler surprised but delighted the other countries of Europe by telling them he stood for peace. We now know that at the same time he was starting German rearmament, and that his purpose was to win time for this to be achieved. A truer sign of things to come was his withdrawal in October 1933 from the League of Nations and the disarmament conference in Geneva. One of his actions which surprised people at the time was a non-aggression pact with Poland in 1934, since even the previous German government had wanted to recover the lands lost to Poland in 1919. For Hitler this pact had the double advantage of lulling Poland into a false sense of security and of damaging France's alliance with Poland. By 1935 he felt secure enough to announce that Germany would not observe the disarmament clauses of the Treaty of Versailles, that she already had a military air force (the Luftwaffe), and that all young men in Germany would undergo military service.

In March 1936 Hitler frightened his own generals by ordering the army to reoccupy the areas along and to the west of the Rhine from which they had been excluded by the Treaty of Versailles. He sought at the same time to play on the nationalism of his own people and to reassure other countries:

> 'In this historic hour, when German troops are taking possession of their future peacetime garrisons in Germany's western provinces, we unite to testify to two holy innermost articles of faith.
>
> First, to the oath to yield to no power or force in the re-establishment of the honour of the nation.
>
> Secondly, to the affirmation that we shall now all the more work for European understanding and particularly for an understanding with the Western powers and our Western neighbours.
>
> After three years I believe that I can regard the struggle for German equality as concluded today.'

Hitler's generals thought that France would surely reply by invading Germany and that they would not be strong enough to resist. A few isolated figures in Britain and France, such as Winston Churchill, said that force should be used before Germany got any stronger. However, Hitler's uncanny understanding of his opponents' weaknesses told him that he could get away with it. The French government was in a particularly weak political position at this time. In addition there was an understandable horror in Britain and France of another war which might match the slaughter of 1914–18 and a fairly general feeling of guilt about the Treaty of Versailles. Many French and British people thought that Germany had been harshly treated in 1919 and that all she was now doing was to send troops into her own territory. What reasonable person could complain about that? Hitler also still believed that Britain would not oppose him in Europe if he did not interfere with her overseas empire and foreign trade. In the event, no action was taken against Germany, and Hitler was confirmed in all these views.

Despite his promise in 1936 that the struggle for German equality had been completed, Hitler was by November 1937 planning to extend the Reich to include Austria and the German-speaking areas of Czechoslovakia. He met his military chiefs and foreign minister, and told them what they were to prepare for. The 'Hossbach Memorandum' (a record made by one of the officers there) has become famous and was used in the trials of Nazi war criminals after the Second World War. Hossbach noted that Hitler said:

> 'The aim of German policy was to make secure and to preserve the racial community and to enlarge it. It was therefore a question of space . . . Germany's problem could only be solved by means of force and this was never without risk . . . Our relative strength would decrease in relation to the rearmament which would by then have been carried out by the rest of the world. If we did not act by 1943–45 we might have a food crisis [because of lack of space]. We were obliged to take the offensive while the rest of the world was still preparing its defences . . . It would of course be necessary to maintain a strong defence on our western frontier during our attack on the Czechs and Austria.'

There has been much argument about what exactly this document means. What is clear is Hitler's characteristic vagueness about a timetable. In the event he acted quickly. In March 1938 German troops marched into Austria to unite it with the Reich. The 'Anschluss' (as it was called) had been forbidden by the Treaty of Versailles, but Britain and France took no action on the grounds that a majority of Austrians welcomed it.

Hitler now accelerated the pace of events either to take advantage of the weakness of the 'appeasers' in the western governments or because he was afraid of being overtaken in rearmament. In September 1938 he demanded that the German-speaking areas round the western frontier of Czechoslovakia (the Sudetenland) should be handed over to Germany. France was bound by treaty to defend Czechoslovakia, which was one of the most successful of the new states created in 1919. But the western powers did not wish to act for what the British prime minister, Neville Chamberlain, called 'a far away country of which we know nothing'. Leaders of the European powers went to see Hitler at Munich and agreed that Germany should have the Sudetenland (and also that Poland and Hungary should have the pieces of

Fig 8.9 Chamberlain inspecting a Nazi guard of honour in Munich in 1938.

Czechoslovakia which they demanded). Figure 8.9 shows Chamberlain at Munich inspecting a Nazi guard of honour. He was soon proclaiming 'Peace in our time'.

It has been claimed that at Munich Chamberlain was really buying time for Britain to rearm. Whatever the truth was, Hitler took it as a sign of weakness and in March 1939 occupied the remaining part of Czechoslovakia. Now there could be no doubting his intentions. Britain promised to defend Poland (which it was clear was Hitler's next target). Either Hitler did not believe that Britain would act, or he decided after recent events that she was too weak to act effectively. He invaded Poland on 1 September 1939, and Britain and France declared war on Germany. They did little to defend Poland, which may have confirmed Hitler's hopes, but the Second World War had started, and in due course it was to bring the downfall of the Nazi state (and the deaths of many millions of people).

The events surrounding the outbreak of war in 1939 have been used to support the arguments of those who believe that Hitler had no long-term plan. He went to war with Britain, whose friendship he had for years said he wanted. A week earlier he had made a ten-year non-aggression pact with the Soviet Union (the 'Molotov-Ribbentrop Pact'). He thus seemed to be making friends with the communist government which he had for so long preached against. However, the pact with Russia expressed no friendship on either side. For Stalin it brought the Baltic states and the eastern part of Poland into the USSR, and it gave Russia time to build up her armaments. For Hitler it brought the western part of Poland (when it had been conquered) into Germany and a chance to avoid a war on two fronts, which is what had overcome Germany in the First World War. After the fall of France in 1940 Hitler hoped that he could make peace with Britain. The emphatic refusal of this offer by Churchill (now the British prime minister), did not deter Hitler from pursuing what had been his ultimate aim throughout – the final show-down with the Soviet Union. On 22 June 1941 his army of 5.5 million men invaded Russia to provide the living space which was to sustain the German people for a thousand years. In fact it led Germany to defeat and Hitler to suicide in 1945.

The ultimate irony was that this arch-German nationalist and Bolshevik-hater paved the way for an era of over forty years when Germany was divided, and when the Soviet Union bestrode the world as one of two great superpowers.

ESSAY

Choose one of the following views about Hitler and the Nazi state, and write an essay to discuss it.

1. 'The Germans of the 1930s cannot really be blamed for Hitler's misdeeds. They were either tricked into agreeing by propaganda or terrorised by Hitler's police state.'
2. 'There is one simple explanation why Germans in the 1930s supported Hitler. He got them back to work.'
3. 'Hitler and the Nazis failed to fulfil two of their principal aims. They neither created a monolithic state nor altered the structure of society by displacing the traditional ruling class.'
4. 'Hitler's foreign policy simply carried forward the aims German nationalists had pursued since the nineteenth century. There was little that was new about it.'

Extended essays

The extended essay is intended as an opportunity to provide evidence of investigating skills such as:

- the ability to identify an issue and place it in context;
- the ability to select and organise information from a variety of sources;
- and the ability to present the findings in a form that shows some attempt at analysis.

The period of German history examined in this book provides good opportunities for selecting an extended essay. Many books have been written in English at different levels and it is possible to study a wide variety of primary sources in translation.

A good starting point in selecting a topic for an extended essay is to look at the questions posed at the beginning of each chapter and the essay titles given at the ends of each chapter in this book. These raise the questions which historians have most often discussed and on which, therefore, it should be easy to find resources.

Often the title of the extended essay will take the form of a question. You may wish to consider one of these questions:

1. A consideration of the importance of an individual in historical developments. This period of German history includes two particularly dominant personalities – Bismarck and Hitler. Essay titles could be:

a) How important was the part played by Bismarck in the unification of Germany?

b) How far did Hitler carry out between 1933 and 1945 policies which he had worked out in the early 1920s and publicised in 1923 in *Mein Kampf*?

2. An evaluation of the reasons for particular events, for example:

Why did the Weimar Republic fail?

3. A discussion of the relationships between political events and the context provided by social, economic, military, or other world affairs, for example:

a) What part did rapid social change at home play in the decisions of William II's governments to pursue aggressive foreign policies and to enter the First World War?

b) What part did the Great Depression play in the rise of Hitler and the Nazis?

4. An evaluation of the reasons for the nature and effectiveness of particular policies, for example:

What were the reasons for the foreign and colonial policies pursued by Bismarck between 1871 and 1890, and how successful were these policies?

Bibliography

The following books may help you to research an extended essay chosen from this period of German history. They are just a few of the many available. They are arranged by type rather than by topic because many of them cover a considerable part of or even all of the period, and cover many possible topics.

Brief accounts useful as a starting point for your further reading

Gibson R, Nichol J 1985 *Germany* Basil Blackwell. This is an outline account of twentieth-century Germany.

Gorman M 1989 *The Unification of Germany* Cambridge University Press Topics in History Series.

Shreeves W G 1984 *Nationmaking in Nineteenth Century Europe – The National Unification of Italy and Germany 1815–1914* Nelson Advanced Studies in History.

Styles A 1986 *The Unification of Germany 1815–1890* Hodder and Stoughton Access to A-Level Series.

Tampke J 1988 *Twentieth Century Germany – Quest for Power* Nelson.

Waller B 1985 *Bismarck* Basil Blackwell Historical Association Studies.

Detailed histories of Germany covering all or most of the period

Carr W 1969 *A History of Germany 1815–1945* Edward Arnold.

Craig G 1981 (paperback edition) *Germany 1866–1945* Oxford University Press.

Mann G 1990 *The History of Germany Since 1789* Penguin.

Detailed studies of parts of the period or topics within it

A detailed bibliography of *Germany 1860–1918* by V R Berghan may be found in *The Historian*, No. 15, Summer 1987, The Historical Association.

Bessel R ed. 1987 *Life in the Third Reich* Oxford University Press.

Berghan V R 1987 *Modern Germany – Society, economy and politics in the twentieth century* 2nd edn Cambridge University Press.

Kershaw I 1991 *Hitler* Longman Profiles in Power Series.

Nicholls A J 1991 *Weimar and the Rise of Hitler* 3rd edn Macmillan.

Collections of extracts from primary sources

Bohme H 1971 *The Foundation of the German Empire* Oxford University Press.

Medlicott W N, Coveney D K 1971 *Bismarck and Europe* Edward Arnold.

Noakes J, Pridham G 1974 *Documents on Nazism, 1919–1945* Jonathan Cape.

Rohl J C G 1970 *From Bismarck to Hitler* Longman Problems and Perspectives in History Series.

Simon W M 1968 *Germany in the Age of Bismarck* George Allen and Unwin.

Index

Acknowledgements

We are grateful to the following for permission to reproduce copyright material:

Basil Blackwell Ltd for adapted extracts from *Bismarck* by Bruce Waller; Cambridge University Press for adapted extracts from *Modern Germany* (2nd edition 1987) by V. R. Berghan; Harper Collins Publishers for the poem 'The German Fatherland' trans. E. Kedourie in *Nationalism* (Hutchinson, 1960); Hodder & Stoughton Ltd for adapted extracts from *A History of Germany 1815–1945* by Wiliam Carr & *Bismarck & Europe* edited and trans. by W. N. Medlicott & Dorothy K. Coveney; Macmillan London & Basingstoke for adapted extracts from *Weimar and the Rise of Hitler* (3rd edition 1991) by A. J. Nicholls; Authors' Agents for adapted extracts from *Documents on Nazism, 1919–1945* (Cape, 1974), edited and translated by Jeremy Noakes and Geoffrey Pridham; Oxford University Press for adapted extracts from *The Foundation of the German Empire* (1971), edited by E. Boehme, trans. Agatha Ramm; Random Century Group for Chatto & Windus for adapted extracts from *The History of Germany Since 1789* by Golo Mann, trans. Marian Jackson; Routledge on behalf of Allen & Unwin for adapted extracts from *Germany in the Age of Bismarck* by W. M. Simon; Rutgers University Press for adapted extracts from *Documents of German History* edited by Louis L. Snyder. Copyright © 1958 by Rutgers, The State University.

We are also grateful to the following for permission to reproduce photographs:

Altonaer Museum, Hamburg, page 109; Bildarchiv Preussicher Kulturbeisitz, Berlin, pages 22, 29, 44, 49, 65, 69, 73, 74, 85, 91, 96, 100, 106 and 131; British Library, pages 8, 13 and 17; Cassell's Illustrated History of the War Between France and Germany, London, 1871–2, page 63 below; Historisches Museum der Stadt, Wien, page 20; Illustrated London News Picture Library, pages 36, 37, 51, 55, 63 above and centre, 111, 116, 117, 119, 123, 131, 133, 158, 159, 171, 175, 187, 192 above, 193 and 201; Jugend, page 107; Friedrich Krupp GmbH, page 77; Magnum Photos, page 5 (photo Rene Burri); Sachsische Landesbibliothek, Dresden, page 31; Suddeutscher Verlag Bilderdientst, Munich, pages 66, 90, 125, 143, 147 above, 155, 156, 184 and 192 below; Ullstein Bilderdienst, Berlin, pages 84, 139 and 147 below.

Cover photographs: The proclamation of William I as the German Emperor (right) from Bildarchiv Preussicher Kulturbeisitz, Berlin; members of the Hitler Youth (left) from Suddeutscher Verlag Bilderdientst, Munich.